# Modern Hand Stitching

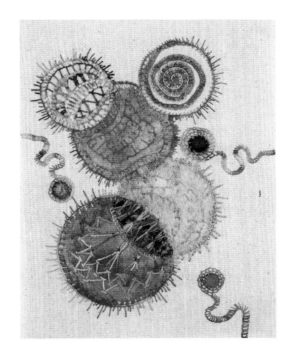

*by Ruth Chandler*

Landauer Publishing

# Modern Hand Stitching

*by Ruth Chandler*

Landauer Publishing, *www.landauerpub.com*, is an imprint of Fox Chapel Publishing Company, Inc.

Editor: Jeri Simon
Art Director: Laurel Albright
Photographer: Sue Voegtlin

Library of Congress Control Number: 2013950340
ISBN: 978-1-935726-48-7

We are always looking for talented authors. To submit an idea, please send a brief inquiry to acquisitions@foxchapelpublishing.com.

Printed in Singapore
21 20 19 18     2 4 6 8 10 9 7 5 3

# Introduction

Modern Hand Stitching is more than just a stitch library. My goal is to encourage you to allow yourself freedom from all the rules and change your perception about hand stitching.

I began hand stitching at the age of 4 while living in Japan, where perfection was the goal. I no longer stitch this way; it is stifling to me. I want to have fun and use stitching as a way to create and relax. I never use a pattern, but instead let the fabric and whimsy dictate the stitching.

There are 38 stitches and dozens of variations in this book. This by no means covers all the stitches in the world, but these are the ones I go back to and use again and again. The stitches are simple to learn and once you learn them you own them. Once you own them you can change them to fit your work.

Modern hand stitching, to me, is synonymous with no rules or boundaries, simple and fun, stress-free and relaxing. I want you to experience the same passion I have for stitching without any rules. If you can't quite grasp this, watch a child with a needle and thread or any art form. Catch the fever of their abandonment to explore and create without rules. My grandchildren have been such an inspiration to me. They don't say, "I can't do that, it is wrong". They just create! It is why I love to teach children. As adults, we have a difficult time remembering and retaining that freedom.

Here are a few things I constantly remind my students and myself:

Anything can be used for thread or fiber. My granddaughter Bethanne wanted to know if you could roll doll filling up into a "string and stitch with it". I immediately said, "let's try and see". It didn't work well but it was fun to try. See, no boundaries!

Change the weight of your thread or fibers often and in the same stitches. I like to start with a heavy thread and work down to a thin one or vice versa.

Layer the stitches. There is no rule that says you can't overlap stitches. Layering gives great depth and texture, especially if the weight of the fiber or thread is varied.

Vary the size of the stitches. Yes, it's ok if they are not all the exact same size! This will give more interest and it takes away the stress.

Distort the stitches. They do not have to all be the same shape. Uneven stitches are much more interesting. Take a look at nature, no two leaves, rocks, clouds, or trees are the same so why would our stitches need to be?

Don't ever forget to ask, "what would happen if I stitched like this?" I have so many happy what ifs.

Take a walk and look closely at everything. There are shapes and textures everywhere that can be recreated with a stitch. It's really eye opening, plus you get a walk.

Keep a journal of ideas, shapes, and textures. I call it my stitch book even though there are no stitches in it. It will become your inspiration.

Let this book of stitches become your inspiration, your permission to forgo any rules or boundaries and stitch with freedom and abandon.

*Ruth*

# Table of Contents

# Table of Contents

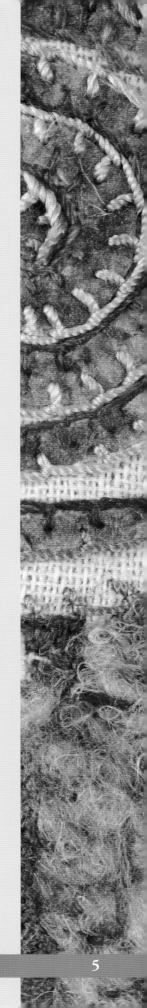

# Supplies

Hand stitching does not require many supplies, but you will soon discover that fibers and threads are just as addictive as fabric or beads. In this section I have listed some of the tools you will need to begin your hand stitching adventure. I have noted which are my favorites, but experiment to see which tools work best for you.

## Thimbles

A thimble will become an important tool once you get in the habit of using it. While many stitchers do not use a thimble, I find one especially useful when stitching with heavier, bulkier threads and fibers. It may take some practice but soon you will be wondering how you stitched without a thimble.

Thimbles can be made from plastic, leather, latex, silver and other metals. They are also available in a variety of styles and price ranges. Take the time and effort to find one that is comfortable for you. It took me approximately 3 years to find my perfect thimble—a heavier silver thimble with the top cut away.

## Needles

Good quality needles are a must for hand stitching. If you do not invest in good quality needles you will be constantly breaking, bending and throwing them away in frustration. There are several brands of quality needles available, such as Clover, John James of England and BohinFrance. Piecemakers® needles are also found in most quilt stores. All are good choices. I was thrilled recently to find Tulip® brand needles in the United States. I grew up using these and love them. Personally, I use Clover gold eye needles. It is easier to thread the gold eye and the quality is the best I have found. I have rarely broken or bent them and they stay sharp.

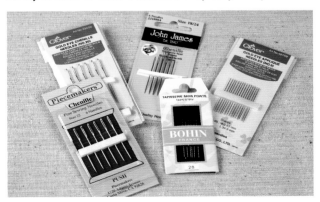

Needle sizes can be confusing at first. Embroidery needles come in sizes 1-10 with 10 being the smallest. They are sharp and have an elongated eye for floss. A chenille needle is thicker and comes in sizes 13 to 26 with size 26 being the smallest. It can be a challenge to find the smaller sizes, so stock up when you do come across them. A chenille needle has a large long eye, a sharp point and is great for hand stitching. Sharps and appliqué needles are finer and have a smaller eye. They come in sizes 1 to 12. They tend to bend more easily due to the fact that they are thinner. These needles are used for finer threads and fabrics.

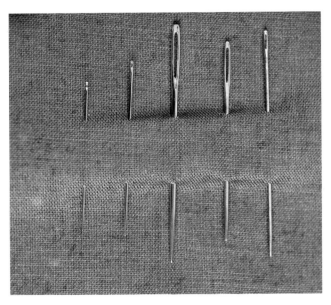

The fabric and fiber choice determine which needle I use. If the fabric is a tight weave, I use a sharp or appliqué needle. If the fabric is a looser weave, I use a chenille or embroidery needle. Sometimes it is a trial and error process. If you have to fight to get the thread or fiber through the fabric, change needles until you find one that works. If it takes more than two or three tries to thread the needle, switch to a larger one. There is no hard and fast rule for which needle to use. The needle should be the same width as the fiber—the thicker the fiber, the bigger the needle.

# Threads and Fibers

Threads and fibers personalize your work and make it come alive, which is why we love to stitch with them. I encourage you to think outside the box and consider non-traditional fibers, such as paper, metal, wire, spools of sewing thread and some yarns and ribbons, for hand stitching. My rule of thumb: if I can't pull it through the fabric easily with a needle, I couch it on. I have used fibers or threads in my work that were never intended to be stitched with and the result has been wonderful. Keeping an open mind will make your work interesting, fun and uniquely yours.

# Floss

Floss is generally sold in yardage that has been folded into a hank. You will want to carefully rewind the floss onto a piece of cardboard or a card purchased for this purpose. The purchased cards are available in paper or plastic. I prefer the plastic ones because they tend to last longer and don't bend.

Floss comes in strands ranging from 4-12 strands per hank. These can be pulled apart and used separately or together. The number of strands you use will be determined by the project you are creating. Cut the strands the length needed before separating them. Separate one strand from the cut length and pull it out. Continue to pull out one strand at a time until you have the number needed. If you try to pull more than one strand at a time, you could end up with a knotted up mess and have to start again.

Cotton floss is the most common and the least expensive type of floss. It is available in virtually any color, as well as hand dyed and variegated. Some brands and colors are more colorfast than others. If you plan to wash your piece test your floss for colorfastness.

Silk floss feels wonderful and can add a touch of sheen to your piece. It is great to work with but is probably the most expensive floss available. Before making a large investment, try mixing silk floss with other fibers for a stunning result. I especially love the variegated silk floss, which can be subtle or very noticeable. Either way, the results are great.

Wool floss is heavier and can be difficult to find. Since it is heavier, it is a good choice to add lots of texture with fewer stitches. It is especially beautiful in primitive work.

Rayon floss is very slick, but has the most shine. While it is a bit more difficult to work with, it is well worth the effort. I suggest working with shorter lengths of floss, as rayon tends to ravel and come apart as you stitch.

Metallic floss tends to be rough and a bit scratchy. It does not feel good against your skin so keep that in mind when using it. It tends to ravel and can sometimes be hard to thread. You may need to use a needle with a larger eye. A little goes a long way and can add a real punch to your project. Remember my rule, if it's difficult to stitch with, couch it on.

# Pearl Cotton

Pearl cotton comes in small balls. Some companies, such as Tentakulum, package pearl cotton in a hank. The size of the pearl cotton is marked on the end of the ball. The thicker the pearl cotton, the smaller the number. For example, a size 8 is thicker than a size 12. Pearl cotton comes in a huge selection of colors, as well as variegated and hand-dyed. Unlike floss, pearl cotton is not meant to be separated. Valdani has a wonderful selection and the hand-dyeing is exquisite.

## Threads

All machine threads should be considered for hand stitching. If the color and weight are right, use it. Machine threads work well for hand stitching and can be stitched individually or in many layers. Mix a variety of threads together to get a perfect combination.

## Fibers

Fibers are categorized as anything that isn't a floss, pearl cotton or thread. This is the perfect place to look for unconventional things to stitch and couch.

I have found spools of metal thread so thin that you can stitch with it. These were not metallic threads, but actual metal. It did kink but it was fun to use.

Paper is a fun fiber choice. I have been fortunate to find a ball of paper, similar to yarn, that I used for couching. Paper will not hold up to pulling through fabric but it makes a great texture to couch.

Yarn comes in many sizes, including some fine enough to use for stitching. One of my personal favorites is a variegated bamboo yarn. It is fine enough to pull

through fabric and is very soft. Another favorite is raw silk yarn. It has to be couched on and gives a totally different look than the silk floss or pearl cotton. Search your favorite yarn store for new fibers to try.

Specialty fibers are any of the beautiful, non-traditional fibers you find. These types of fibers are not usually smooth and can be difficult to pull through fabric. Some have loops and nubbies that won't allow you to stitch with them. If this the case, couch with them or use a looser weave fabric such as Osnaburg. You will be glad you did.

Gimp is a cotton cord wrapped with nylon and works great for couching. It holds its shape just enough to make it easy to couch. The gimp comes in variegated hand dyes from Tentakulum. I have yet to find another company that sells gimp.

## Scissors

A good pair of sharp scissors are a must when hand stitching. You don't want a dull scissors that gnaws at your threads instead of cutting them. A good clean thread cut will allow you to thread your needle with minimal frustration. Cut your thread or fiber at an angle to make it easier to thread. I use scissors from Havel's® because of the variety of blades available, as well as the sharpness. I keep several different pairs with my stitching. It is important to use the right tool with the right thread or fiber.

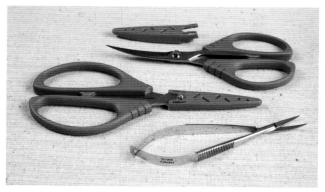

## Fabric

You can hand stitch on any fabric; some are just easier than others. Generally the looser the weave, the easier it is to pull the needle and thread through the fabric. For example, batik and silk fabrics have a tighter weave and would need a sharper, finer needle than wool or cotton.

## Miscellaneous supplies

Needle grabbers are small round rubber disks that come 2 or 3 to a package. They are used to grab and pull the needle through a tight or particularly tough spot. Needle grabbers are wonderful and inexpensive tools.

Magnetic needle holders come in many sizes and styles. These are essential for keeping your needles in one place. If you drop a needle, simply wave the magnetic needle holder around the area and it will pick it up. How cool is that?

Fabric marking pencils are available from a variety of manufacturers. I prefer the mechanical pencil type. The lines are very fine and the lead is available in several colors.

Good lighting is a must when it comes to hand stitching. I do a lot of my handwork in the evening and have a large OttLite® over my chair. Eyestrain is not worth it; invest in a good light.

Reading glasses are with my stitching at all times. It may seem like an odd 'tool' to list, but glasses make a huge difference for me when trying to thread a needle or work on a stitch.

Carry along tote allows you to take your project with you when traveling. Hand stitching is wonderfully portable and can easily be carried with you anywhere. Choose a tote with lots of pockets to keep your stitching organized. Or, better yet, make your own tote.

A comfortable chair is priceless and it will allow you to stitch longer.

## Take Along Stitch Kit

*When you are ready to hit the road, pack these essentials in your stitch kit.*

- Stitching project
- Threads and fibers for project
- Needles - several sizes and types
- Needle grabber
- Thimble
- Scissors
- Fabric marking pencil
- Glasses
- Band-Aids
  (no one wants blood on their work)
- Tweezers
- Hand lotion
- Fingernail file
- Chocolate

# Stitch Play

Create a stitch sampler book to practice your stitches before embarking on a larger project. The sampler book is also a great reference tool that you will go back to again and again.

## Making a Stitch Sampler Book

13" x 43" piece of neutral fabric (I used Osnaburg from Roc-Lon® because it has a looser weave)

13" x 43" piece of batting

Neutral thread for sewing machine

Small scissors

Fabric marking pencil

Sewing machine

Pins

Optional: Hoop

*I personally do not use a hoop, but do what is most comfortable for you.*

*Note: If you are not making the sampler book, be sure to stabilize your fabric with batting. This will keep the fabric from bunching up as you hand stitch. There are a number of stabilizers available that can also be used. I do not recommend a paper stabilizer as it can be difficult to hand stitch through.*

## Getting started

**1** Press the fabric to remove any wrinkles or creases. Using the fabric marking pencil, draw a line lengthwise through the middle of the fabric.

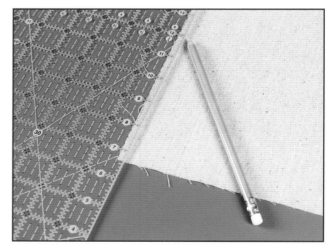

**2** Beginning at one end of the fabric, mark a 1/4" seam allowance line along the width. Continue to mark a line every 4-1/2" along the width of the fabric. There will be a few extra inches on the opposite end that will be cut off when the book is finished.

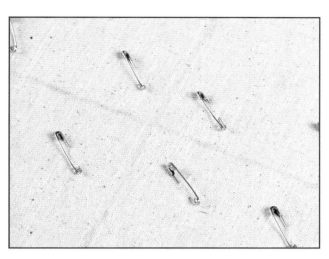

**3** Layer the fabric and batting and pin.

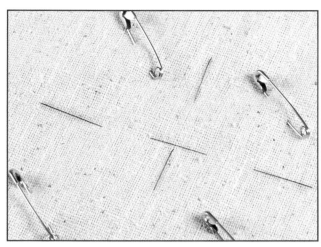

**4** Using a hand or machine basting stitch, sew on the marked lines. This stitching will form the sections for each page of the stitch sampler book.

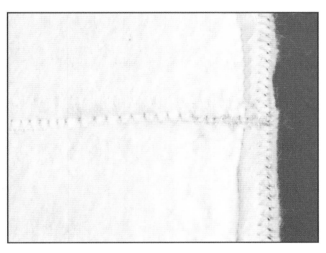

**5** Using a zigzag stitch, stitch around the raw edges of the fabric and batting to prevent raveling.

*Note: If you are not creating the stitch sampler book, cut a piece of batting or stabilizer slightly larger than the fabric you are stitching on. Layer the fabric and batting and pin around all edges. Machine stitch around all edges using a straight or zigzag stitch. Begin hand stitching.*

You should now have a layered fabric rectangle with 2 rows of 4-1/2" sections for a total of 18 sections. This is the base of the book and all the stitching will be done on this piece.

Before beginning to hand stitch, mark the lower right section of the stitch sampler book. This will be the front of the book. Do not use this section for a stitch.

Stitches used include blanket stitch, buttonhole stitch, cross stitch, backstitch, satin stitch, French knots, detached cross stitch and open chain stitch.

Stitches used include stem stitch,
backstitch, cross stitch and couching.

# Straight Stitches

Straight stitches are simple stitches. The variations occur by using different lengths and placements of the stitch. These stitches appear simple but there are many variations that can be achieved by slight changes in the placement of the needle in the fabric. Straight stitches are used to achieve line. They can be used to outline, fill in, and give the illusion of direction. For example, curved straight stitches used in a tree will invoke the suggestion of the wind blowing.

*The piece on page 16 provides a glimpse of a little pond with cherry blossoms and a few cattails. Valdani threads were used throughout the entire piece. Pearl cotton, bits of silk, and lots of hand-dyed cheesecloth add texture to the scene. A hint of silk ribbon gives the water a little sparkle.*

# Straight Stitch

The straight stitch is the simplest and quickest stitch to learn. However, the length and direction of the stitch can make it appear more complicated. Think of it as a zigzag with the "zig" on the top of the fabric and the "zag" underneath.

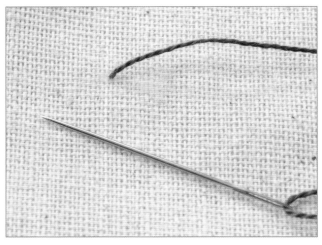

**1** Thread the needle and knot the thread. Bring the needle and thread up from the back of the fabric to the front.

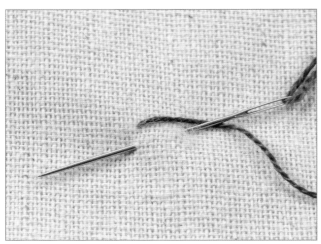

**2** Insert the needle down into the fabric where you want the first stitch to end. Bring the needle and thread back up to the top of the fabric at the beginning of the second stitch.

*Note: Remember to keep the needle on top of the fabric while stitching. Working on top of the fabric will limit the number of stitch motions needed, as well as reduce hand fatigue.*

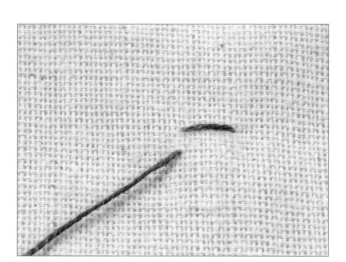

**3** Exit the fabric all in one motion, keeping the needle on top of the fabric. Do not pull the stitch too tight or it will cause the fabric to bunch.

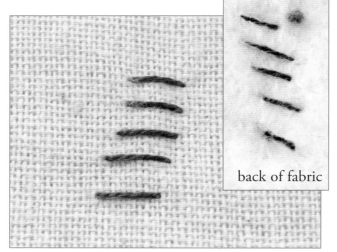

back of fabric

**4** Continue stitching in the same manner. When you are finished stitching, take the needle and thread to the back of the fabric and knot. There will be stitches on the back of the fabric similar to the stitches on the front.

# No Boundaries

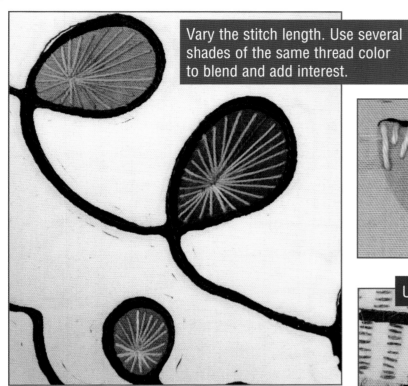

Vary the stitch length. Use several shades of the same thread color to blend and add interest.

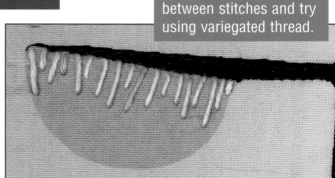

Vary the spacing between stitches and try using variegated thread.

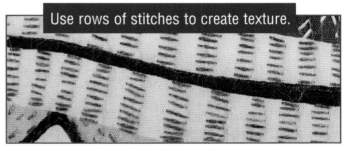

Use rows of stitches to create texture.

Vary the weight of the thread.

For a large area, use several rows of straight stitches to avoid loose stitches.

## Tips

- Hold the fabric as flat as possible when stitching to avoid bunching.

- The straight stitch uses a lot of thread. Take this into consideration when planning to stitch a large area.

- The straight stitch is a great way to draw attention to an area without overwhelming it.

- Grass and greenery fill-in are a great way to use the straight stitch.

# Running Stitch

The running stitch is a straight stitch worked in a line. The spaces between the stitches and the stitch length are the same. This stitch is used in the Japanese technique of Sashiko. Think of this stitch as a dotted line.

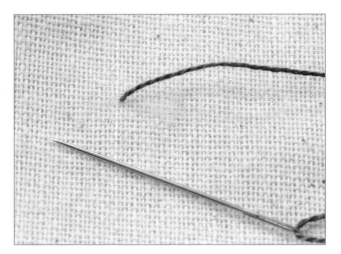

**1** Thread the needle and knot the thread. Bring the needle and thread up from the back of the fabric to the front where you want to begin stitching.

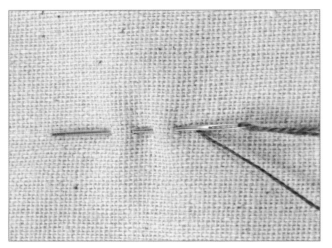

**2** Keeping the needle on top of the fabric, bring the needle in and out of the fabric loading 3-4 stitches on it. Make the stitches and the spaces between stitches equal in length.

**Note:** *Remember to keep the needle on top of the fabric while stitching. Working on top of the fabric will limit the number of stitch motions needed, as well as reduce hand fatigue.*

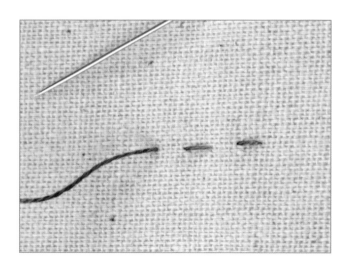

**3** Pull the needle and thread through the fabric. Take care not to pull the thread too tight.

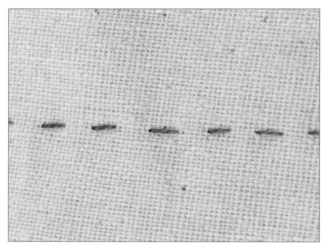

**4** Continue stitching in the same manner. When you are finished stitching, take the needle and thread to the back of the fabric and knot.

# No Boundaries

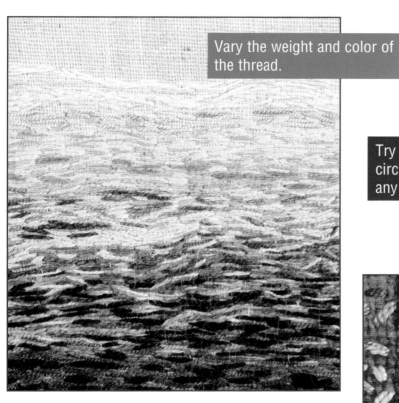

Vary the weight and color of the thread.

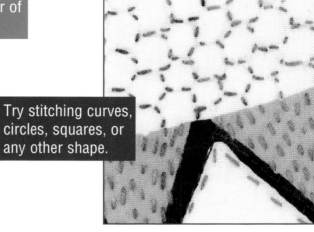

Try stitching curves, circles, squares, or any other shape.

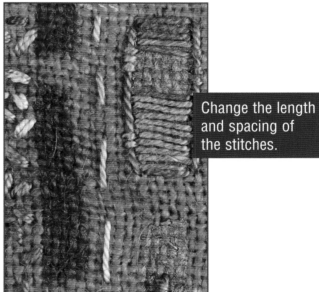

Change the length and spacing of the stitches.

Use the running stitch to outline an area to make it stand out.

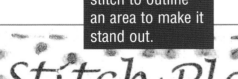

## Tips

- This is not a quilting stitch so you will not 'rock' the needle.

- Use heavier threads for a more primitive look.

- It is very important to keep the fabric flat and not to pull the thread too tight.

# Backstitch

The backstitch is worked backward, just as the name implies. It is a good substitute for the straight stitch, especially if working in a large area because it uses less thread. The backstitch also gives the look of a straight solid line as opposed to the running stitch, which resembles a broken line.

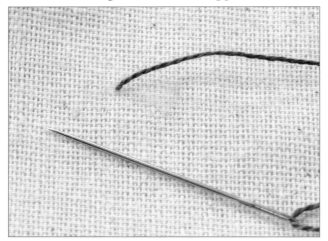

**1** Thread the needle and knot the thread. Bring the needle and thread up from the wrong side of the fabric.

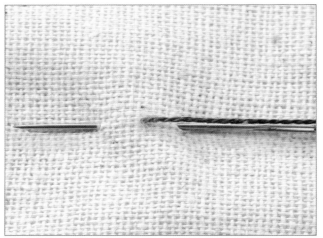

**2** Keep the needle on top of the fabric and work right (back) to left (front). Insert the needle one stitch length to the right, or behind, and bring it up one stitch length to the left, or in front, of where the thread exits the fabric.

*Note: Remember to keep the needle on top of the fabric while stitching. Working on top of the fabric will limit the number of stitch motions needed, as well as reduce hand fatigue.*

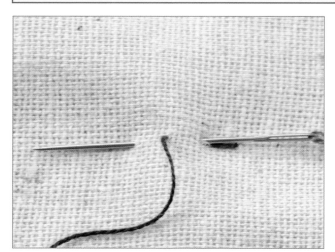

**3** Pull the needle and thread through the fabric to create a stitch. Insert the needle in the end of the stitch and exit one stitch length to the left, or in front, of the thread. This is a two steps forward and one step back motion.

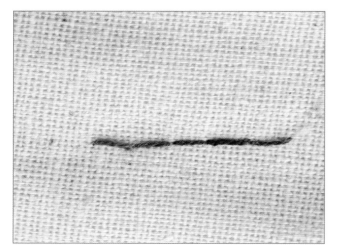

**4** Continue stitching in the same manner until the design is complete. When you are finished stitching, take the needle and thread to the back of the fabric and knot.

# No Boundaries

Bring the needle up and split the thread of the previous stitch. It will look similar to a chain stitch.

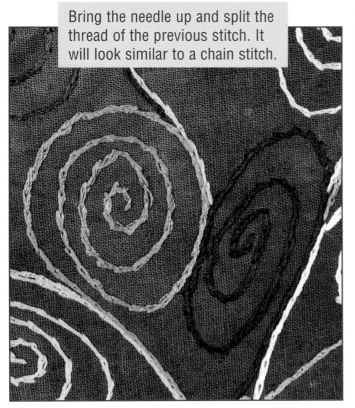

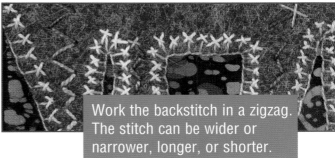

Work the backstitch in a zigzag. The stitch can be wider or narrower, longer, or shorter.

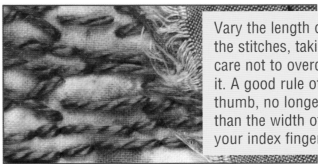

Vary the length of the stitches, taking care not to overdo it. A good rule of thumb, no longer than the width of your index finger.

Backstitching works well for creating letters and numbers.

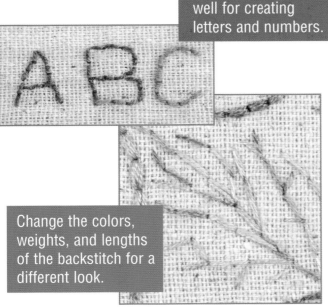

Change the colors, weights, and lengths of the backstitch for a different look.

## Tips

- Enter the stitch as close to the exit of the previous stitch as possible to get a better solid line.

- Don't make the stitches too long or you will lose the line and it will resemble a group of straight stitches.

- Backstitch around a print or appliqué to make it appear more prominent.

- It takes a little extra time to make sure the needle enters the fabric at the exact end of the previous stitch, but it is worth the effort to get a straight line.

- Use smaller stitches when curving a line.

# Stem Stitch

The stem stitch is similar to the backstitch, but the needle is brought up above and beside the stitch. The stem stitch is typically used for flower stems but is a very versatile stitch. It has a fuller, thicker appearance than the backstitch, making it easy to create many variations.

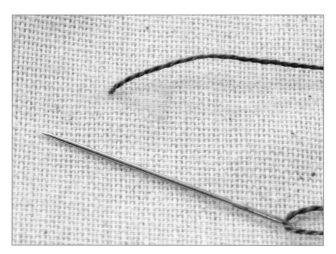

**1** Thread the needle and knot the thread. Bring the needle and thread up from the wrong side of the fabric where you want to begin stitching.

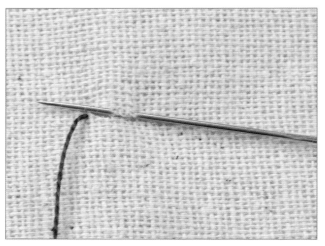

**2** Take the needle tip down into the fabric and come up just above and to the right of the thread exit. Pull the needle and thread through the fabric to create the first stitch.

*Note: Remember to keep the needle on top of the fabric while stitching. Working on top of the fabric will limit the number of stitch motions needed, as well as reduce hand fatigue.*

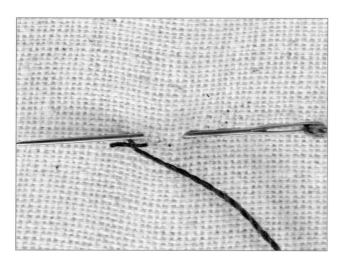

**3** For the second stitch, insert the needle one stitch length to the right of the first stitch, bringing the needle halfway up and beside the first stitch.

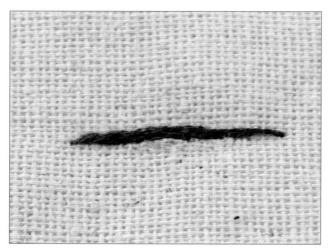

**4** Continue stitching in the same manner until the design is complete. When you are finished stitching, take the needle and thread to the back of the fabric and knot.

# No Boundaries

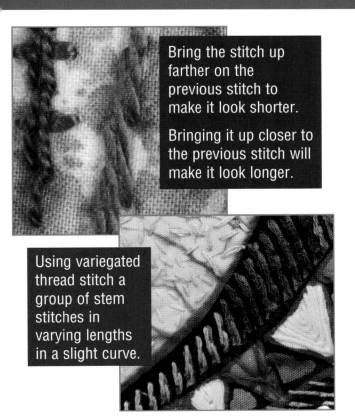

Bring the stitch up farther on the previous stitch to make it look shorter.

Bringing it up closer to the previous stitch will make it look longer.

Using variegated thread stitch a group of stem stitches in varying lengths in a slight curve.

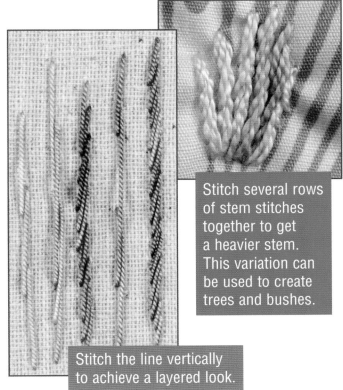

Stitch several rows of stem stitches together to get a heavier stem. This variation can be used to create trees and bushes.

Stitch the line vertically to achieve a layered look.

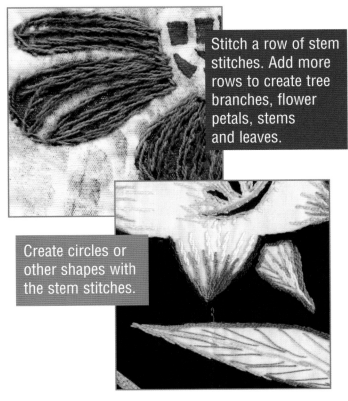

Stitch a row of stem stitches. Add more rows to create tree branches, flower petals, stems and leaves.

Create circles or other shapes with the stem stitches.

## Tips

- Stay as close to the previous stitch as possible without being under it.

- The stem stitch can be used to create a thick heavy line.

- The stem stitch can be stitched under the first stitch instead of above it. It is your choice.

- To stitch curves, use small stitches. As the line curves change from stitching above to below the previous stitch.

# Ricing Stitch

The ricing stitch is basically a short running stitch. It is sometimes called a scatter or seed stitch. The most difficult thing about this stitch is keeping it random. Try to avoid falling into a pattern while stitching. A few ricing stitches are often the 'little something else' a piece needs, or they can be the star of the show. The stitches should not be more than 1/4" to 1/3" long. Keep the stitches compact so they don't catch on fingers, thimbles or other items while working.

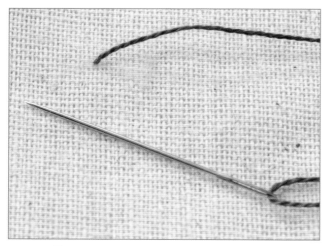

**1** Thread the needle and knot the thread. Bring the needle and thread up from the back of the fabric to the front where you want to begin stitching.

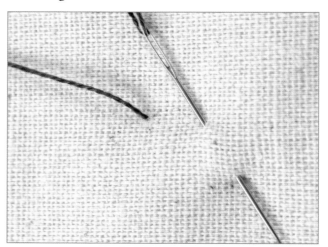

**2** Keeping the needle on top the fabric, take a 1/4" to 1/3" stitch in any direction. Bring the needle up where you want the next stitch to begin.

> *Note:* *Remember to keep the needle on top of the fabric while stitching. Working on top of the fabric will limit the number of stitch motions needed, as well as reduce hand fatigue.*

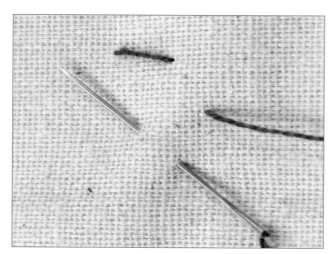

**3** Pull the needle and thread through and take another stitch in another direction keeping the stitch length fairly consistent.

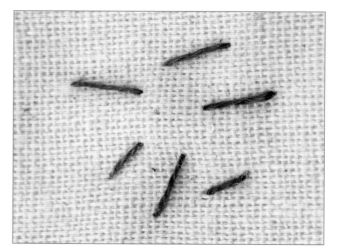

**4** Continue stitching in the same manner until the area is covered. When you are finished stitching, take the needle and thread to the back of the fabric and knot.

# No Boundaries

Use different thread weights in the same colorway to fill a background with ricing stitches.

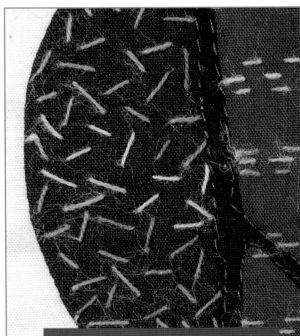

Use variegated thread or threads in complementary colors to fill an open space.

Use a variety of lengths when creating your ricing stitches.

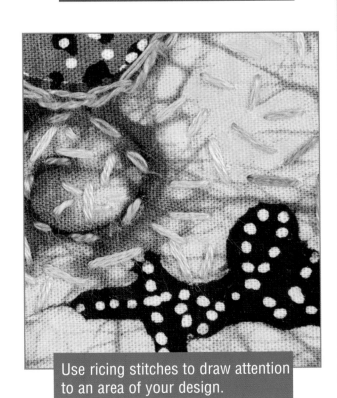

Use ricing stitches to draw attention to an area of your design.

# Satin Stitch

The satin stitch is a series of straight stitches butted up next to each other. Satin stitches are commonly used to create a solid all over look. The stitch is perfect for flowers, leaves, or any design that needs to be filled in.

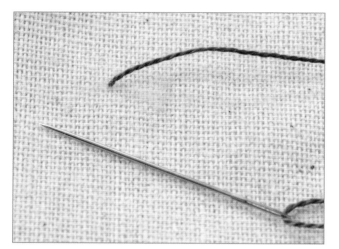

**1** Thread the needle and knot the thread. Bring the needle and thread up from the back of the fabric to the front where you want to begin stitching a design.

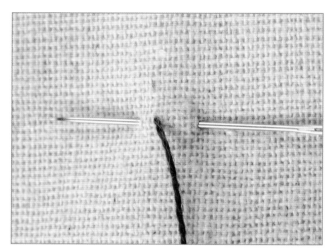

**2** Insert the needle down into the fabric where you want the first stitch to end. Bring the needle and thread back up to the top of the fabric and lined up as close to the first stitch as possible.

> *Note: Remember to keep the needle on top of the fabric while stitching. Working on top of the fabric will limit the number of stitch motions needed, as well as reduce hand fatigue.*

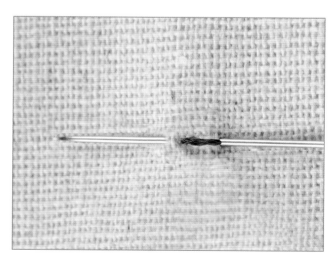

**3** Pull the needle and thread through the fabric to create the first stitch and begin the second.

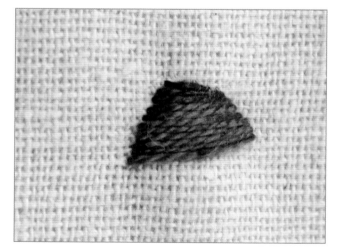

**4** Continue to line up your stitches as closely as possible until the design has been filled in. There should not be any fabric visible through the threads.

# No Boundaries

Stitch the satin stitch farther apart to make it easier to go back and fill in with other threads.

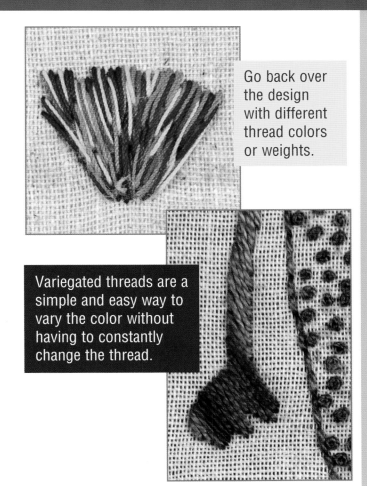

Go back over the design with different thread colors or weights.

Variegated threads are a simple and easy way to vary the color without having to constantly change the thread.

Vary the length of the stitches, then go back and fill in to add more texture.

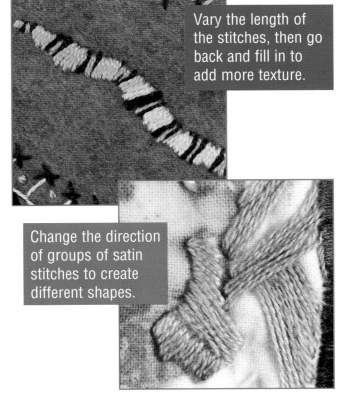

Change the direction of groups of satin stitches to create different shapes.

## Tips

- Use a fabric marking pencil to draw the shape or design onto the fabric before stitching to make it easier to fill in.

- Do not pull the threads too tight or the fabric will bunch up.

- The design should look the same on the front and back.

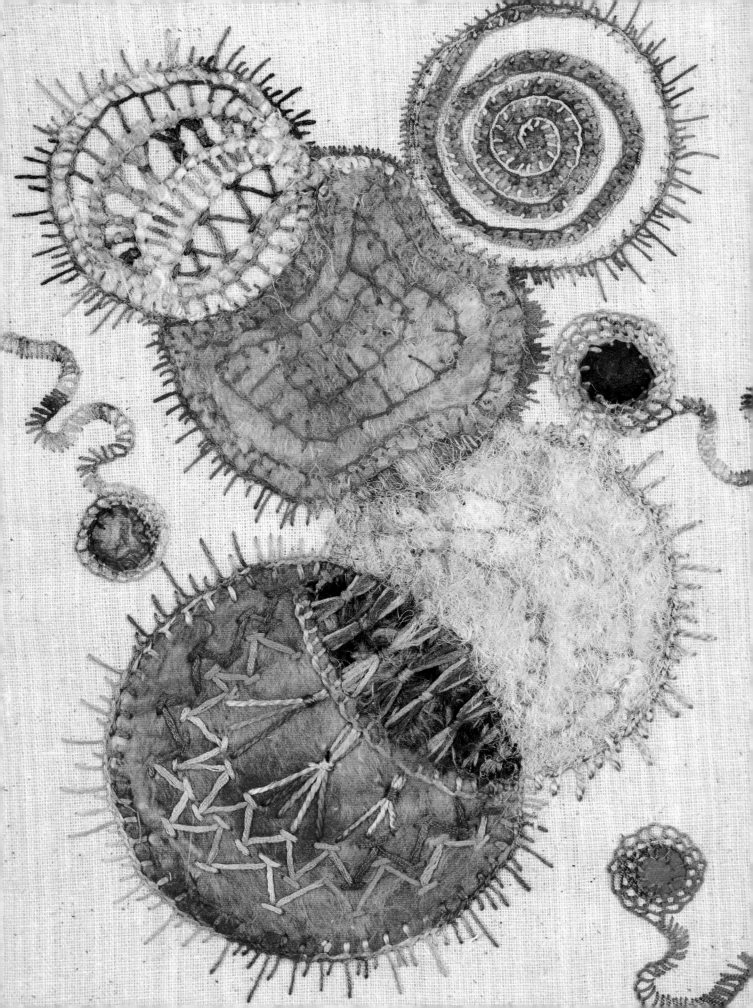

# Building Stitches

The stitches in this section build on the elements of the straight stitch from section 1. They are still relatively simple to stitch while creating L, V, and X shapes.

*The piece on page 30 began with an Inspiration Pack from Treenway Silks and a challenge on Textile Evolution to use it. Circles are one of my favorite shapes to stitch and became the focal point of the piece. Silk hankies, roving, cocoons, and rods were arranged and then stitched down with Treenway's wonderful threads and floss.*

# Blanket Stitch

The blanket stitch resembles a chain of L's or half a ladder. Use it on the edge of a blanket to give it a nice finished look. In other areas it can be a fence or used to anchor an area.

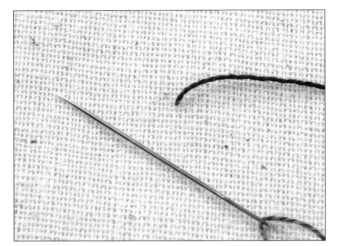

**1** Thread the needle and knot the thread. Bring the needle and thread up from the back of the fabric to the front where you want to begin stitching.

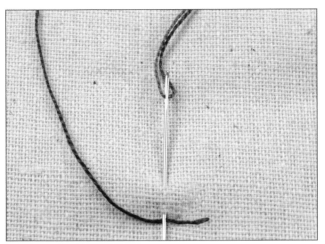

**2** Insert the needle where you want the first stitch to end. Exit approximately 1/4" in front of the beginning of the first stitch at a right angle, keeping the thread under the tip of the needle.

> *Note:* *Remember to keep the needle on top of the fabric while stitching. Working on top of the fabric will limit the number of stitch motions needed, as well as reduce hand fatigue.*

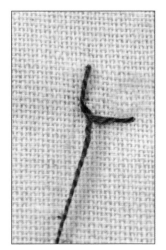

**3** Pull through to make the first L.

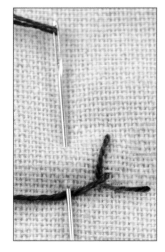

**4** Continue stitching in the same manner.

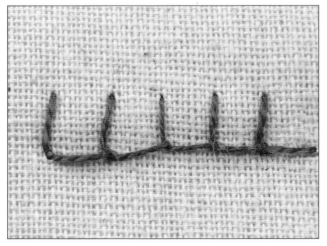

**5** When you are finished stitching, take the needle and thread to the back of the fabric and knot.

# No Boundaries

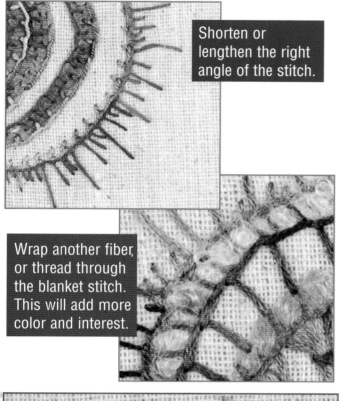

Shorten or lengthen the right angle of the stitch.

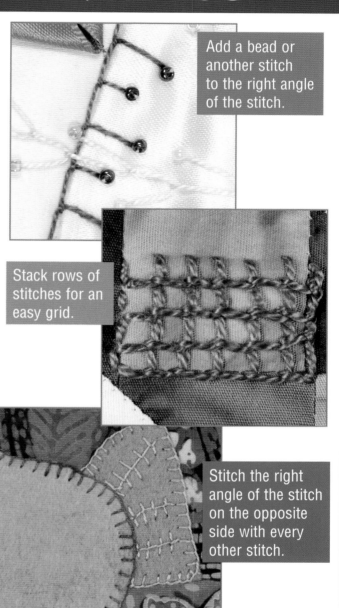

Add a bead or another stitch to the right angle of the stitch.

Wrap another fiber, or thread through the blanket stitch. This will add more color and interest.

Stack rows of stitches for an easy grid.

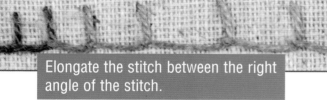

Elongate the stitch between the right angle of the stitch.

Stitch the right angle of the stitch on the opposite side with every other stitch.

Vary the elongated section to give an undulating look.

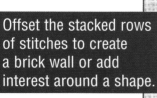

Offset the stacked rows of stitches to create a brick wall or add interest around a shape.

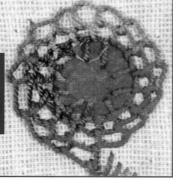

## Tips

- Use the blanket stitch on raw edges to help prevent fabric from fraying.
- Use your thumb to hold the looped thread to prevent tangling.

# Buttonhole Stitch

The buttonhole stitch is a blanket stitch with the stitches worked very close together. It could easily be called a blanket satin stitch. Traditionally, the stitch was used to finish buttonholes before sewing machines became commonplace.

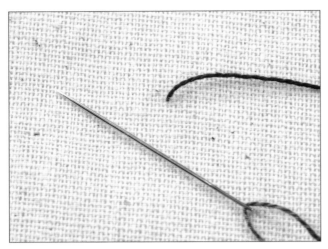

**1** Thread the needle and knot the thread. Bring the needle and thread up from the back of the fabric to the front where you want to begin stitching.

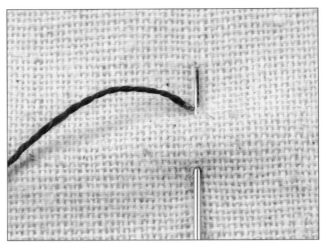

**2** Insert the needle where you want the first stitch to end. Exit at a right angle as close to the first stitch as possible.

> *Note: Remember to keep the needle on top of the fabric while stitching. Working on top of the fabric will limit the number of stitch motions needed, as well as reduce hand fatigue.*

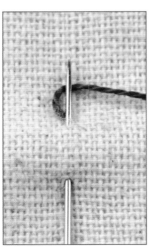

**3** Loop the thread around the point of the needle and pull through. Continue stitching in the same manner.

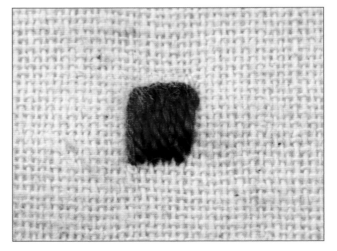

**4** When you are finished stitching, take the needle and thread to the back of the fabric and knot.

# No Boundaries

Lengthen or shorten the right angle of the stitch.

Use the buttonhole stitch to protect raw fabric edges from raveling.

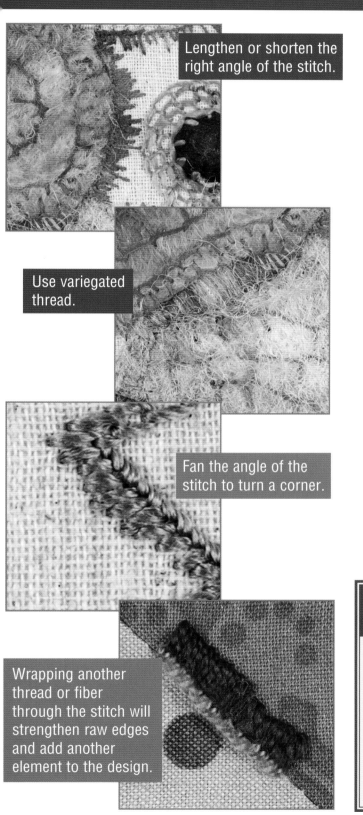

Use variegated thread.

Fan the angle of the stitch to turn a corner.

Alternate buttonhole stitches with other stitches to outline a shape or motif.

Wrapping another thread or fiber through the stitch will strengthen raw edges and add another element to the design.

## Tips

- The stitches should be so close together that fabric is not visible between stitches.

- Use your thumb to keep control of the looping thread to avoid knotting.

- Keep the stitches even and tightly spaced to insure any raw edges will not ravel.

# Sheaf Stitch

The sheaf stitch is a group of long straight stitches drawn up in the center with a small straight stitch. Vertically it resembles a full cross stitch or a sheaf of grain. Horizontally it has the appearance of a bow.

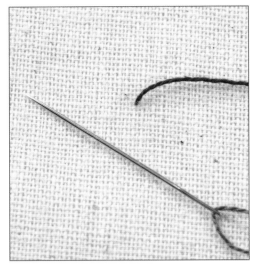

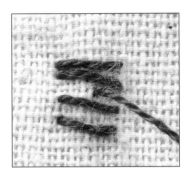

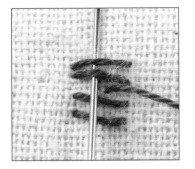

**1** Thread the needle and knot the thread. Bring the needle and thread up from the back of the fabric to the front where you want to begin stitching.

**2** Stitch 3-4 straight stitches of the same length close together. They do not need to be butted up against each other but they do need to be close. When making your final stitch, bring the needle and thread up under the center of the group of straight stitches.

**3** Take the needle and thread to the outside by going under the stitches.

*Note: Remember to keep the needle on top of the fabric while stitching. Working on top of the fabric will limit the number of stitch motions needed, as well as reduce hand fatigue.*

**4** Loop the thread up and over the straight stitches. Insert the needle into the fabric close to the thread exit and pull to draw the straight stitches together. This will wrap the straight stitches and hold them together in the center. Do not pull so tight that the fabric bunches.

**5** Continue creating sheaf stitches in the same manner. When you are finished, take the needle and thread to the back of the fabric and knot. It is not necessary to cut the thread after knotting if the individual stitches are close together.

# No Boundaries

Change the thread for the center loops.

Move the location of the center loop.

Stack the stitches.

Stack and offset the stitches.

Lengthen or shorten the straight stitches to create different size sheaf stitches.

Wrap the stitches with several loops.

Put the wrapped loop close to one end of the straight stitches to create a tassel-like stitch.

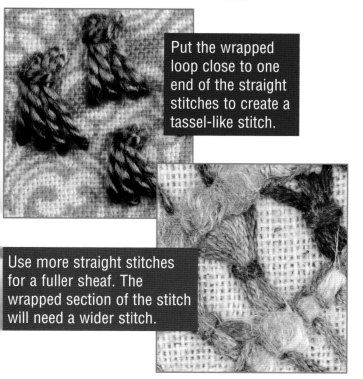

Use more straight stitches for a fuller sheaf. The wrapped section of the stitch will need a wider stitch.

## Tips

- Do not make the straight stitches too long or they could catch and pull when the piece is used.

- The straight stitches may be wrapped more than once.

- Take care not to pull the thread too tight, especially after the last straight stitch.

- Keep the fabric flat while stitching.

# Chevron Stitch

The chevron stitch is a series of backstitches worked horizontally and diagonally. Small backstitches are stitched at the top and bottom of each diagonal. This stitch may seem complicated at first, but once you do it, it will become easy.

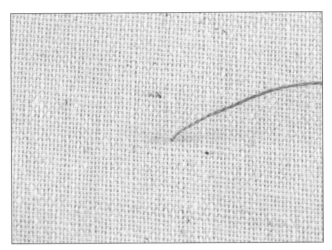

**1** Thread the needle and knot the thread. Bring the needle and thread up from the back of the fabric to the front where you want to begin stitching.

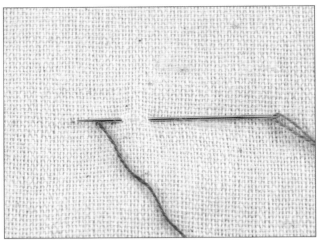

**2** Insert the needle into the fabric approximately 1/4" to the right of the thread exit. Bring the point of the needle up in the center to make a small stitch.

*Note: Remember to keep the needle on top of the fabric while stitching. Working on top of the fabric will limit the number of stitch motions needed, as well as reduce hand fatigue.*

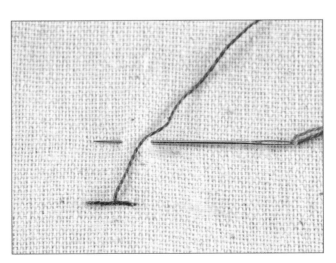

**3** Take a diagonal stitch 1/2" above and slightly to the right of the small stitch, bringing the needle back out 1/8" to the left of the diagonal thread.

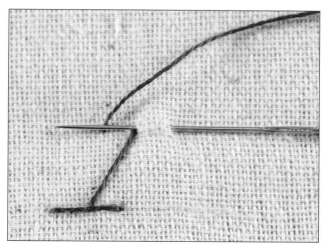

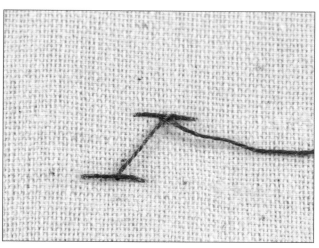

**4** Take a small stitch, approximately 1/8" to the right of the diagonal thread. Bring the point of the needle up where the diagonal thread exits the fabric.

**5** Your stitch should look like a capital I leaning to the right.

*Note:* *Remember to keep the needle on top of the fabric while stitching. Working on top of the fabric will limit the number of stitch motions needed, as well as reduce hand fatigue.*

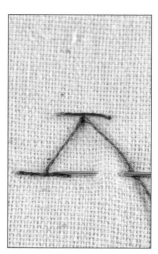
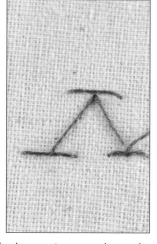

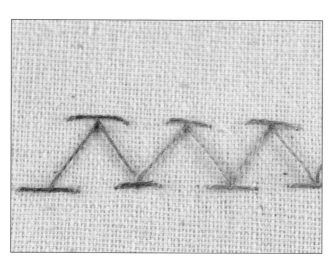

**6** Bring the next stitch down at an angle and slightly to the right, taking a small right to left stitch. Bring the point of the needle up where the diagonal thread exits the fabric. The stitch will resemble an upside down V with small stitches on the top and bottom.

**7** Continue the row of stitches until it is the length desired. When you are finished, take the needle and thread to the back of the fabric and knot.

# Cross Stitches

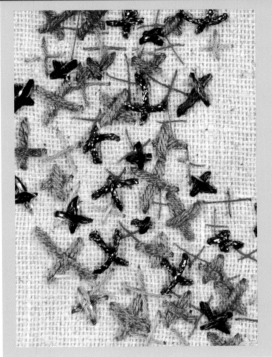

A cross stitch has threads that cross over each other in one form or another. These stitches are often used to fill in a background for an overall design or sprinkled here and there to add interest. There are two basic ways to stitch a cross stitch—in a row or detached. The variations for this stitch are endless. Experiment with thread weights, stitch lengths, and the position of the cross to create a fun and unique piece.

*In Colorado we eagerly await spring and the new growth that signifies the long winter is over. Those spring days are what inspired me to create the piece on page 40. I used several Krienik threads to create layering effect with the stitches. If you look closely you will see a sparkle of metallic threads in the thorn stitches.*

# Cross Stitch in a Row

To cross stitch in a row, use a diagonal stitch to the end of the row. Return to the beginning of the row by stitching in the opposite direction and crossing over the original diagonal stitches.

**Tip**

- Using a fabric marking pencil, draw a top and bottom line showing where to begin and end the stitches. This will make it easier to keep the stitches even and you will be able to stitch more quickly.

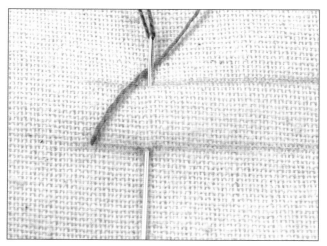

**1** Thread the needle and knot the thread. Bring the needle and thread up from the back of the fabric at the bottom of the row where you want to begin stitching.

**2** Insert the needle into the top of the row to the right of the thread exit below. Bring the needle back up at the bottom of the row at a right angle, forming a diagonal stitch.

*Note: Remember to keep the needle on top of the fabric while stitching. Working on top of the fabric will limit the number of stitch motions needed, as well as reduce hand fatigue.*

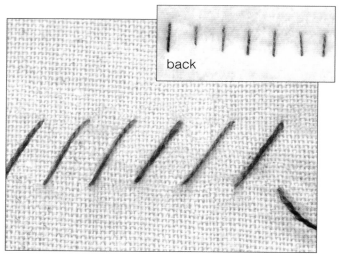

back

**3** Continue to make diagonal stitches until you reach the end of the row. There should be straight stitches on the back of the fabric and diagonal stitches on the front.

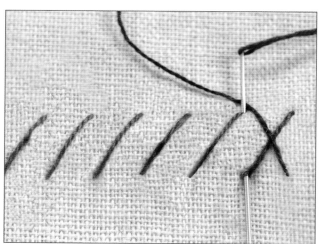

**4** Work back the other direction by inserting the needle down into the top of the stitch closest to the end of the row. Bring the needle back up at the bottom of the final stitch in the row. This will create an X.

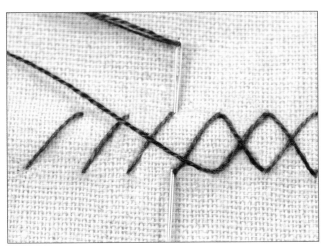

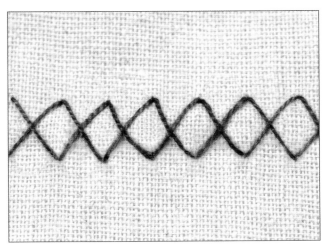

**5** Continue crossing back over the stitches entering and exiting where the thread enters and exits the fabric until the row is complete.

**6** When you are finished stitching, take the needle and thread to the back of the fabric and knot.

# No Boundaries

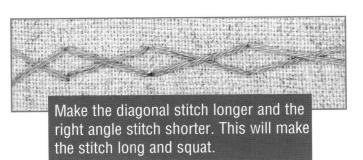

Make the diagonal stitch longer and the right angle stitch shorter. This will make the stitch long and squat.

Try stitching at a right angle instead of a diagonal.

Change one of the stitch lengths. It will draw the cross over to a different place.

## Tips

- Take care not to pull the thread too tight. You want the fabric and stitches to lay flat.

- Use the same stitch technique to create rows of detached X's.

# Detached Cross Stitch

The detached cross stitch is very versatile. It can be uniform or random. The uniform takes a little more effort to keep even, but the random has no rhyme or reason much like the ricing technique.

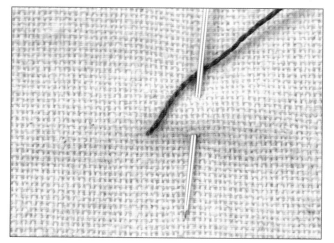

**1** Thread the needle and knot the thread. Bring the needle and thread up from the back of the fabric to the front where you want to begin stitching.

Insert the needle into the fabric above and to the right of the exit thread to create a diagonal stitch. Bring the needle and thread back out of the fabric at a right angle.

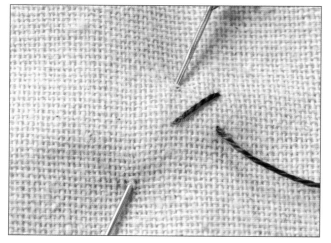

**2** Cross back over the first stitch and insert the needle into the fabric to create an X, while bringing the needle back up where the next stitch is to be placed.

*Note:* *Remember to keep the needle on top of the fabric while stitching. Working on top of the fabric will limit the number of stitch motions needed, as well as reduce hand fatigue.*

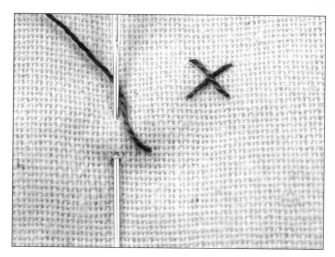

**3** Continue to make detached cross stitches.

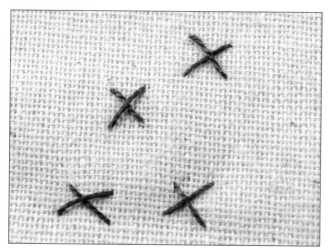

**4** When you are finished stitching, take the needle and thread to the back of the fabric and knot.

# No Boundaries

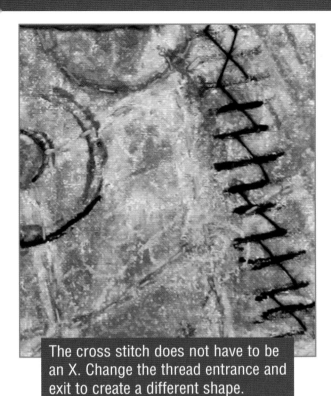

The cross stitch does not have to be an X. Change the thread entrance and exit to create a different shape.

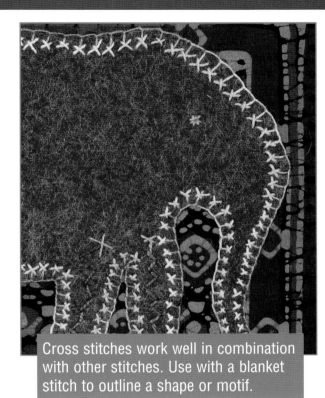

Cross stitches work well in combination with other stitches. Use with a blanket stitch to outline a shape or motif.

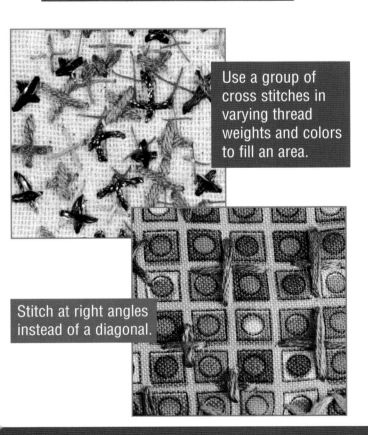

Use a group of cross stitches in varying thread weights and colors to fill an area.

Stitch at right angles instead of a diagonal.

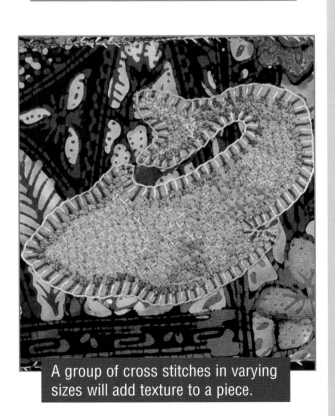

A group of cross stitches in varying sizes will add texture to a piece.

# Herringbone Stitch

The herringbone stitch is a row of cross stitches where the thread crosses closer to the top and bottom instead of the center.

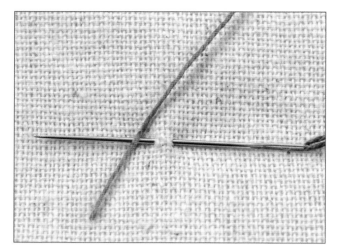 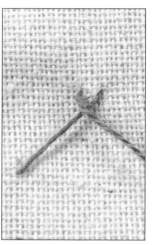 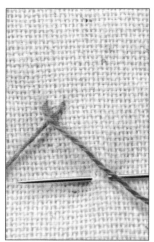

**1** Thread the needle and knot the thread. Bring the needle and thread up from the back of the fabric to the front where you want to begin stitching. Take a small stitch above and to the right of the thread exit.

**2** Bring the needle across the thread and down to the right.

**3** Take another small stitch the same size as the first from right to left.

*Note: Remember to keep the needle on top of the fabric while stitching. Working on top of the fabric will limit the number of stitch motions needed, as well as rreduce hand fatigue.*

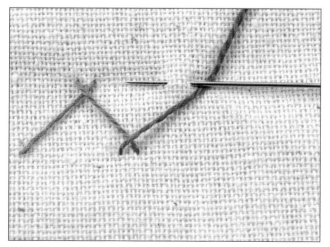 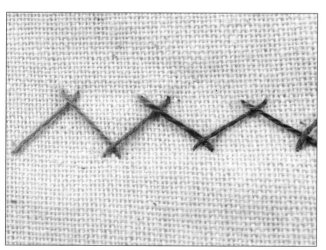

**4** Bring the needle up and cross over the thread. Continue the row of stitches until it is the length desired.

**5** When you are finished stitching, take the needle and thread to the back of the fabric and knot.

# No Boundaries

Make the stitch wide and short.

Detach the stitches instead of keeping them in a row.

Make the stitch tall and narrow.

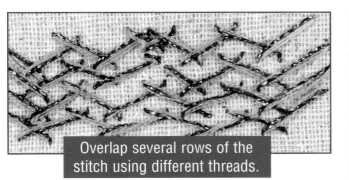

Overlap several rows of the stitch using different threads.

## Tips

- The herringbone stitch is traditionally stitched in a row, but don't make your row too long or it will begin to pucker.

- Since it can be difficult to get these stitches even, mark the top and bottom of the stitch line.

- This is a great stitch to use with thicker threads.

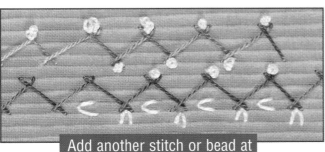

Add another stitch or bead at the top of the stitch.

*Ruth says*

*Widen stitches*

# Feather Stitch

The feather stitch has the appearance of a series of connected V's stitched first one direction and then another. This stitch can cover a large area relatively quickly and easily.

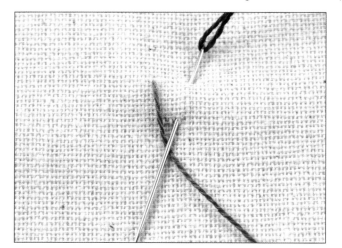 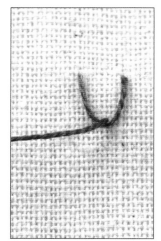 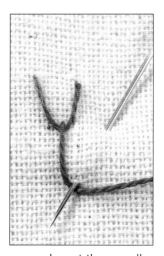

**1** Thread the needle and knot the thread. Bring the needle and thread up from the back of the fabric to the front where you want to begin stitching. Insert the needle approximately 1/4" to the right of where the thread exited the fabric. Bring the needle back up in the center and below the thread exit to form a V.

**2** Loop the thread under the needle and pull through.

**3** Insert the needle approximately 1/4" to the right of the thread exit. Insert the needle in the center and below the stitch to form a V while keeping the thread under the needle.

> **Note:** *Remember to keep the needle on top of the fabric while stitching. Working on top of the fabric will limit the number of stitch motions needed, as well as reduce hand fatigue.*

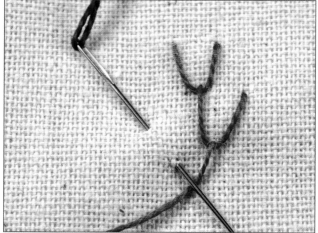 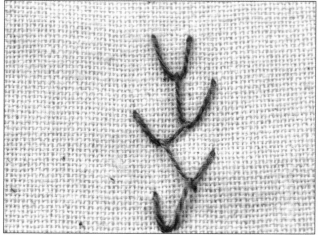

**4** To change directions, simply insert the needle 1/4" to the left of the thread exit. Bring the needle back up in the center and below the stitch to form a V.

**5** Continue stitching, changing directions as desired. When you are finished stitching, take the needle and thread to the back of the fabric and knot.

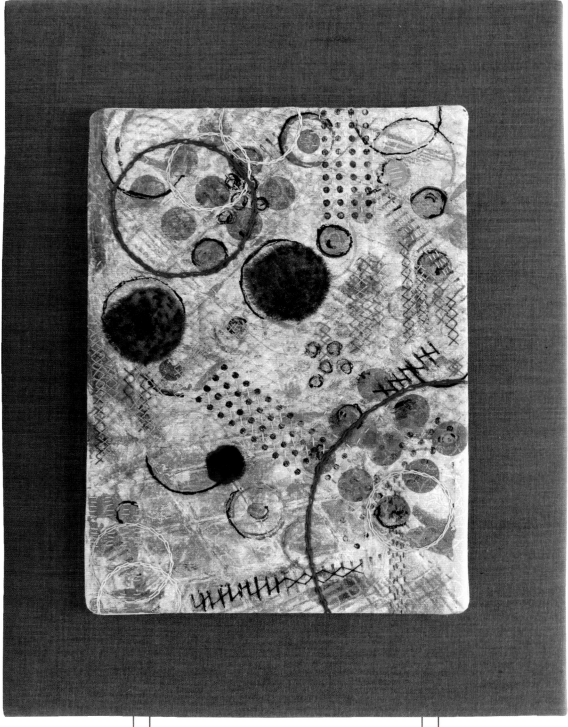

Stitches used include cross stitch, chain
stitch, seed stitch, and straight stitch.

# Detached Feather Stitch

Detached feather stitches are not attached to one another and can be stitched in any direction.

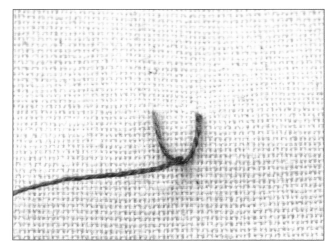

**1** Thread the needle and knot the thread. Bring the needle and thread up from the back of the fabric to the front where you want to begin stitching. Insert the needle approximately 1/4" to the right of where the thread exited the fabric, bringing the needle back up in the center and below the stitch to form a V.

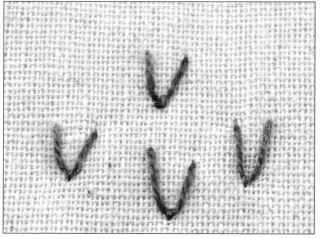

**2** Loop the thread under the needle and pull through.

> *Note:* Remember to keep the needle on top of the fabric while stitching. Working on top of the fabric will limit the number of stitch motions needed, as well as reduce hand fatigue.

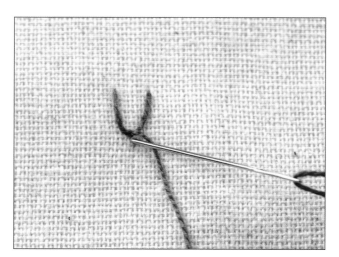

**3** Insert the needle right below the bottom of the V as close as you can to complete the stitch.
*Note:* If the second detached feather stitch is close to the first, bring the needle back up at the beginning of the second stitch instead of taking it completely through to the back.

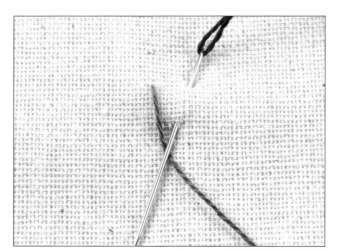

**4** Continue to make detached feather stitches. If the stitches are all in the same area, you can continue stitching and knot when you are finished. However, if they are far apart you may want to knot each one separately.

# No Boundaries

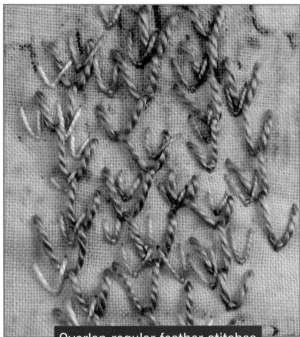

Overlap regular feather stitches with detached stitches.

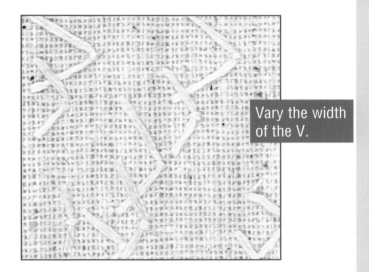

Vary the width of the V.

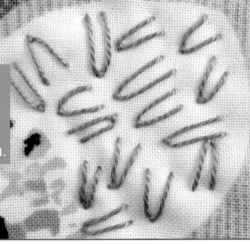

Space the bottom of the V farther below to create an elongated stitch.

Vary the length and width of the stitches to make them irregular.

## Tips

- The detached feather stitch will cover large areas, singly or in a row.

- Create a zig-zag look with the stitch. The zig and zag sections do not need to be the same length.

- The detached feather stitch is great to use for covering a large area.

# Fly Stitch

The fly stitch looks like a Y and is very similar to the feather stitch. It is not attached like the feather and can have a tail that is very short or long.

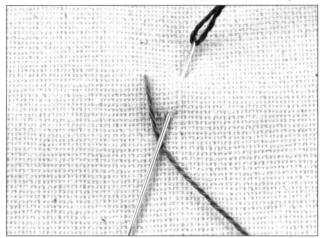

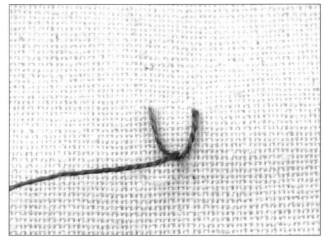

**1** Thread the needle and knot the thread. Bring the needle and thread up from the back of the fabric to the front where you want to begin stitching. Insert the needle approximately 1/4" to the right or left of the thread exit. Bring the needle back up in the center and below the stitch to form a V.

**2** Loop the thread under the needle and pull through.

---

*Note: Remember to keep the needle on top of the fabric while stitching. Working on top of the fabric will limit the number of stitch motions needed, as well as reduce hand fatigue.*

---

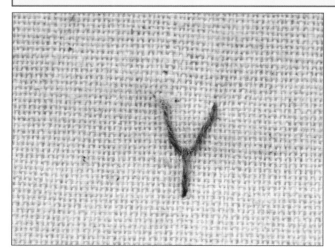

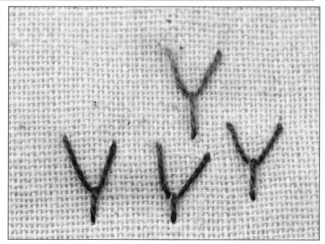

**3** Insert the needle 1/4" below the V to form a Y.
*Note: If the second fly stitch is close to the first, bring the needle back up at the beginning of the second stitch instead of taking it completely through to the back.*

**4** Repeat to make another stitch. If the stitches are all in the same area, you can continue stitching and knot when you are finished. However, if they are far apart you may want to knot each one separately.

# No Boundaries

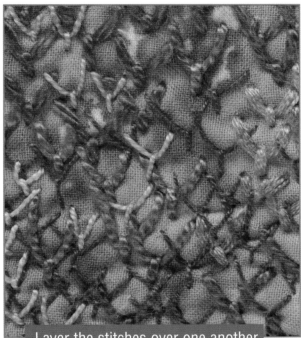

Layer the stitches over one another with different weights of thread.

Change thread colors and layer the stitches.

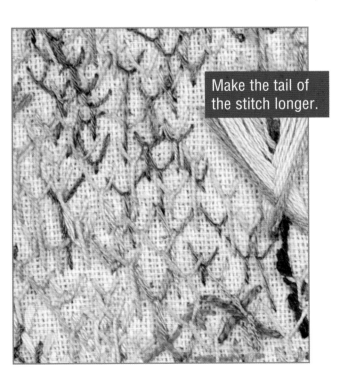

Make the tail of the stitch longer.

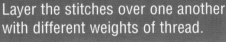

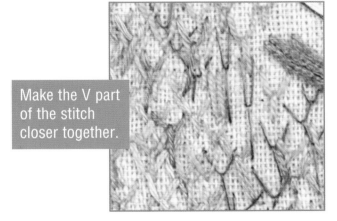

Make the V part of the stitch closer together.

## Tips

- Do not pull the thread too tight.
- There is no size "rule" for the width of the Y or the length of the tail.

# Thorn Stitch

The thorn stitch is seldom used, but fun and easy to make. Individually it can be a focal point, while several together can create a garden or forest. The thorn stitch has a long stitch that uses cross stitches in various lengths and threads to hold it down.

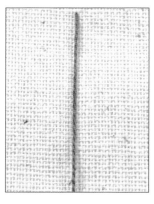

**1** Thread the needle and knot the thread. Bring the needle and thread up from the back of the fabric to the front. Take a 2-3" stitch and knot off under the fabric. Keep this stitch flat and do not pull too tight. This will be the stem.

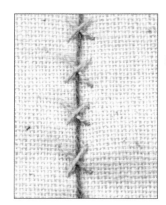

**2** With either the same or a different thread begin making detached herringbone or cross stitches over the stem. Start at the top and work down to the bottom of the stem. These stitches are the thorns.

*Note: Remember to keep the needle on top of the fabric while stitching. Working on top of the fabric will limit the number of stitch motions needed, as well as reduce hand fatigue.*

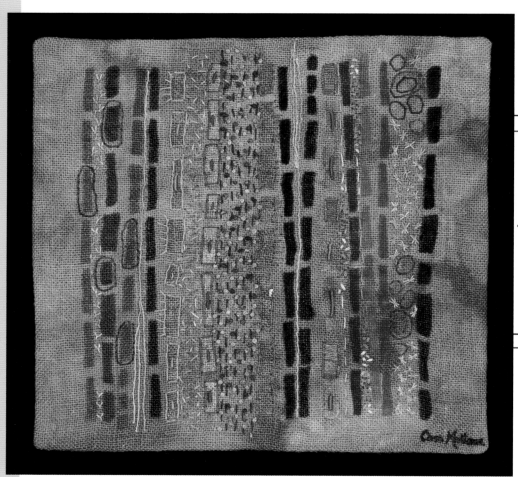

*Designer Gallery*

### Textures 3 by Cass Mullane

Stitches used include straight stitch, running stitch, backstitch, ricing, sheaf stitch, fly stitch, French knot, bullion knot, seed stitch and couching.

# No Boundaries

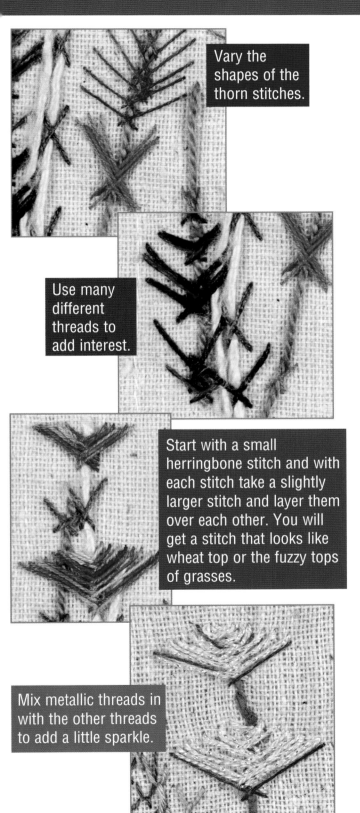

Vary the shapes of the thorn stitches.

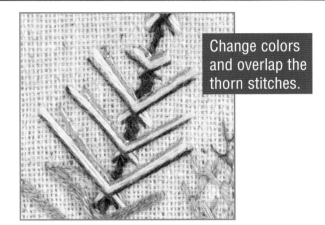

Change colors and overlap the thorn stitches.

Use many different threads to add interest.

Start with a small herringbone stitch and with each stitch take a slightly larger stitch and layer them over each other. You will get a stitch that looks like wheat top or the fuzzy tops of grasses.

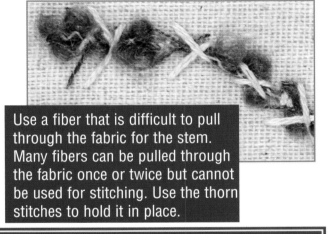

Use a fiber that is difficult to pull through the fabric for the stem. Many fibers can be pulled through the fabric once or twice but cannot be used for stitching. Use the thorn stitches to hold it in place.

Mix metallic threads in with the other threads to add a little sparkle.

## Tips

- Use thinner threads for the thorns and a thicker thread for the stem. This will give more detail and texture.

- Be careful not to pull the stem thread too tight or the fabric will bunch up.

- If you want a stem longer than 3"-4", make several stem stitches so it will lay flat.

- Thin threads will give a wispy look much like dandelion puffs.

- Try leaving the first stitch very loose to allow the stem to curve.

# Wheatear Stitch

The wheatear stitch looks like a chain stitch with a V in the center. It is worked in a row and is very difficult to detach. It gives a layered look without having to change stitches and threads.

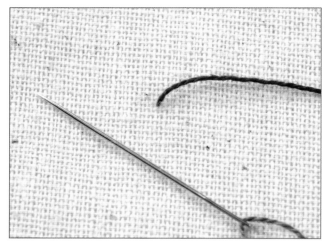

**1** Thread the needle and knot the thread. Bring the needle and thread up from the back of the fabric to the front where you want to begin stitching.

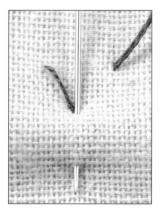

**2** Use a backstitch (page 22) to make a V. Bring the needle back up 1/4" below the bottom of the V.

**3** Take the needle and thread through the point of the V.

---

*Note:* Remember to keep the needle on top of the fabric while stitching. Working on top of the fabric will limit the number of stitch motions needed, as well as reduce hand fatigue.

---

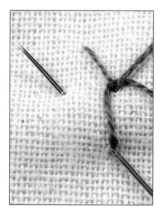

**4** Insert the needle as shown to create a chain stitch. Bring the needle back up where the second V will begin.

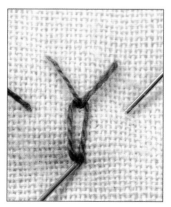

**5** Stitch another V and repeat steps 3 and 4.

**6** Continue stitching in the same manner. When you are finished stitching, take the needle and thread to the back of the fabric and knot.

# No Boundaries

Lengthen the stitch below the V to get an elongated loop.

Use variegated thread for the wheatear stitch.

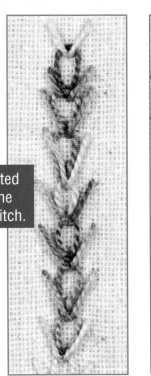

It will require a little more work, but try switching the threads for the loops. To do this you will have to stitch all the V's and then go back and stitch the loops

Use different lengths to form a V in the same row.

## Tips

- It is easier to get an even stitch if the V section of the stitch is consistent.

- Keep the tension even and make sure the loop is not pulled too tight.

- The wheatear stitch requires a lot of looping and pulling, so thick or heavy threads are not recommmended.

*Ruth says* → *Lengthen stitches*

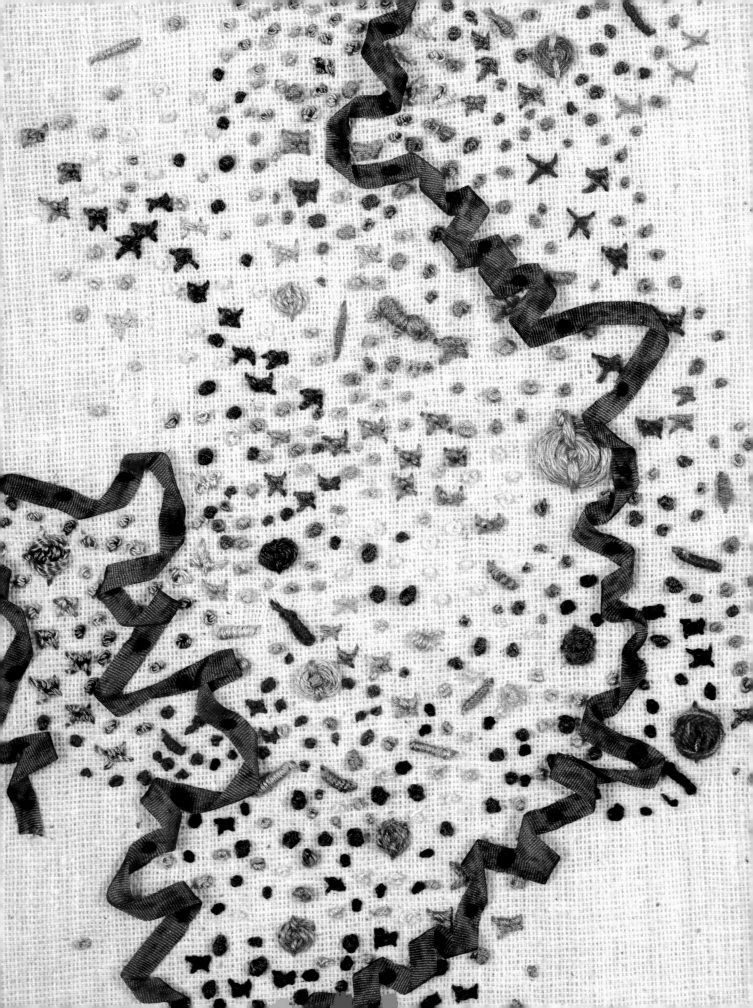

# Knots

Knots are a wonderfully versatile stitch that can add texture to a background or a pop of color to a flower center. They can be a small, simple dot or a large, intricate wrapped cross. The length and width of the knot can be altered by simply changing the number of wraps or thread weight used. Knots may seem challenging at first, but after a bit of practice they will soon become a favorite.

*I love playing with only one type of stitch to create a feeling of movement. In the piece on page 58, I started by stitching several knots, but felt something was missing so I couched the silk ribbon on using small knots. It made a huge visual impact. The ribbon gave the eye a path to follow without overshadowing the knots. A wide range of Tentakulum threads were used with a bit of Valdani pearl cotton in the mix.*

# French Knot

Traditionally, the thread is wrapped around the needle three times to form a French knot. However, the thread can be wrapped around the needle as many times as desired. The more wraps of thread around the needle, the larger the knot. If too many wraps are made it will become very difficult to pull the needle through without losing control of the wrapped thread. When this happens the knot becomes loose and messy.

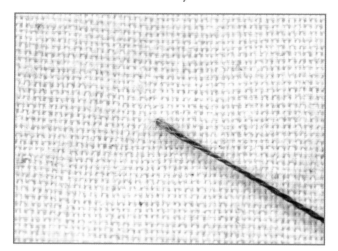

**1** Thread the needle and knot the thread. Bring the needle and thread up from the back of the fabric to the front where you want to place the knot.

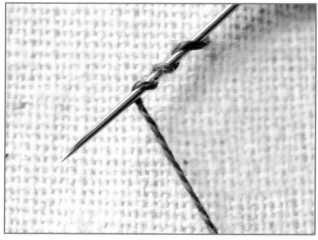

**2** Wrap the thread around the needle 1-3 times.

*Note: When you are stitching the French knot you will need to use your thumb to hold the wraps in place. In order for the stitch steps to show clearly, we did not use hands in the photos.*

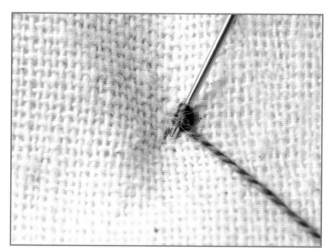

**3** Insert the needle into the fabric as close to where the thread exits the fabric as possible. Slide the wrapped thread down to the fabric with your thumb.

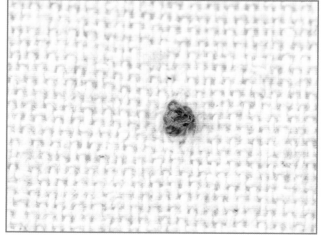

**4** Pull the needle and thread straight through to the back of the fabric. Do not let go of the wrapped thread until it is snugged up to the fabric creating the knot.

# No Boundaries

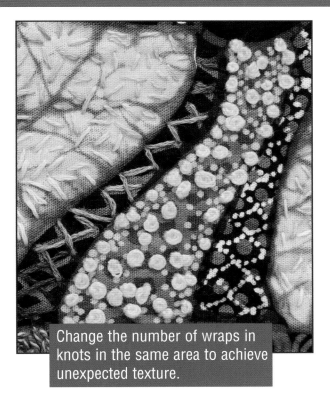

Change the number of wraps in knots in the same area to achieve unexpected texture.

Mix things up. Use different weight threads to get a bigger or smaller knot.

Variegated thread is always a great choice.

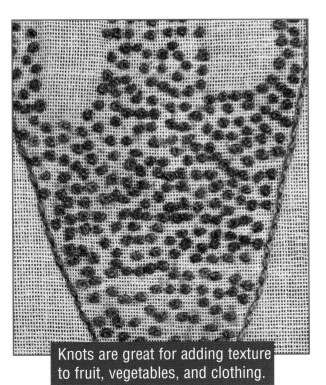

Knots are great for adding texture to fruit, vegetables, and clothing.

## Tips

- A nicer looking knot will be achieved if the thread is kept taut with your thumb.

- The number of wraps as well at the thickness the thread will dictate the size of the knot.

- If the knots are more than 1" apart, knot off each one and start over to prevent puckering.

# Threaded Cross Stitch Knot

The threaded cross stitch knot will make a bigger knot than the French knot. The knot will resemble a flower depending on the choice of thread color.

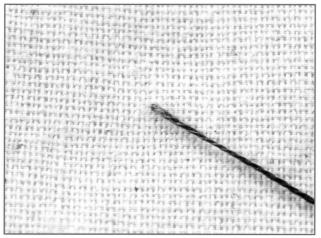

**1** Thread the needle and knot the thread. Bring the needle and thread up from the back of the fabric to the front where you want to begin the stitch.

**2** Stitch a cross. The cross needs to be even on all sides.

*Note: Remember to keep the needle on top of the fabric while stitching. Working on top of the fabric will limit the number of stitch motions needed, as well as reduce hand fatigue.*

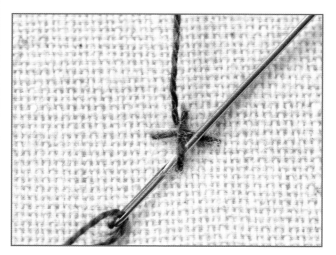

**3** Beginning in the center, weave the thread over and under the spokes of the cross.

**4** Continue weaving until the cross is filled. When you are finished stitching, take the needle and thread to the back of the fabric and knot.

# No Boundaries

Change the threads for wrapping and wrap loosely so the cross shows through.

Make a large cross, but don't fill it in completely. Leave part of the cross showing.

Switch the wrapping and go under where you were going over and then switch back.

Instead of wrapping the whole cross wrap the legs of the cross separately. It will look like 4 bullion knots in a cross.

## Tips

- Make the cross as symmetrical as possible.

- Do not pull the wrapping thread too tight or it will pull the knot out of shape.

- It is easier to get a flat knot if you work on a flat surface.

- The threaded cross stitch knot is a great choice if you need a larger French knot.

*Designer Gallery*
### Pictographs Interpreted by Kerry Cain

Stitches used include straight stitch, backstitch, satin stitch and French knots.

# Bullion Knot

The bullion knot is the knot that many people find confusing. Once you adapt to the concept of working backwards, it will get easier. These knots do use more thread so plan accordingly.

*Note: When you are stitching the bullion knot you will need to use your thumb to hold the wraps in place. In order for the stitch steps to show clearly, we did not use hands in the photos.*

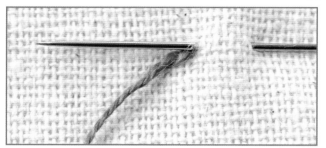

**1** Thread the needle and knot the thread. Bring the needle and thread up from the back of the fabric. Take a stitch to the right of where the thread exited the fabric. Insert the needle back into the fabric where the thread exited.

*Note: Remember to keep the needle on top of the fabric while stitching. Working on top of the fabric will limit the number of stitch motions needed, as well as reduce hand fatigue.*

**2** Wrap the thread around the needle 5-7 times.

**3** Slide the wrapped stitches down the needle and snug them up to the fabric with your thumb.

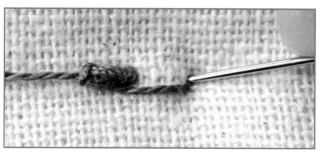

**4** Keeping your thumb on the wraps, carefully pull the thread through the fabric. Insert the needle into the fabric where the thread exited to the right of the wraps. The wraps will pull over to the right when the needle re-enters the fabric.

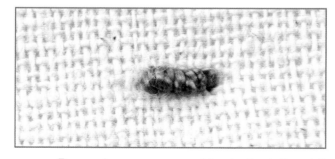

**5** Remember, you are working to the left and then back over to the right. When you are finished stitching, take the needle and thread to the back of the fabric and knot. When you are making a series of bullion knots that are fairly close, there is no need to knot off after each one..

# No Boundaries

Make flowers, bugs, worms or mortar in bricks. The possibilities with this stitch are endless. Let your imagination go.

Use a bullion knot for the tops of wheat or grasses.

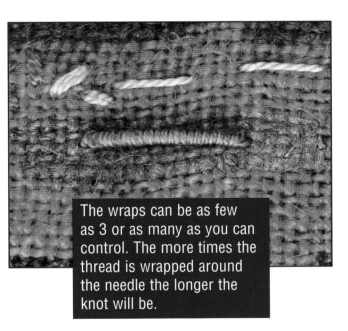

The wraps can be as few as 3 or as many as you can control. The more times the thread is wrapped around the needle the longer the knot will be.

## Tips

- The bullion knot is formed to the left but ends up facing right in the same manner as the backstitch. Time spent practicing will keep you from tearing out threads.

- It will take practice to get the right tension on the wraps—too tight and they won't slide down the eye of the needle, too loose and the knot will be messy.

- Choose a needle with the smallest eye possible to make it easier to slide the thread down and over it.

- The length of the stitch should be as close to the length of the wraps as possible.

- Always choose a contrasting thread for this stitch. Why go to all the work only to have it blend in with the fabric?

- The bullion knot needs to be practiced for it to feel natural. Don't give up, it will add a great look to your piece.

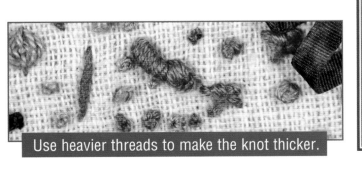

Use heavier threads to make the knot thicker.

# Sorbello Knot

The sorbello knot resembles a cross stitch with a knot in the middle. You don't often see this stitch, but it is a great knot.

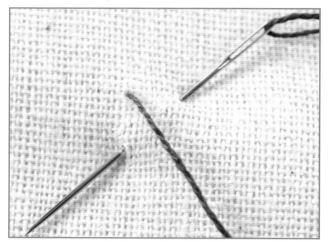 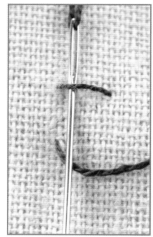 

**1** Thread the needle and knot the thread. Bring the needle and thread up from the back of the fabric. Take a stitch, 1/4" or smaller, directly to the right of where the thread exited the fabric. Bring the needle back up to the front of the fabric approximately 1/4" and directly below the thread exit.

**2** Loop the thread over and through the first stitch keeping the thread under the needle and to the left side of the stitch. Do not pull too tight.

> *Note: Remember to keep the needle on top of the fabric while stitching. Working on top of the fabric will limit the number of stitch motions needed, as well as reduce hand fatigue.*

  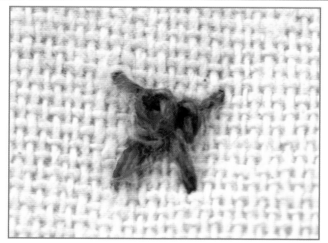

**3** Make another loop through the first stitch keeping the thread under the needle and to the right of the stitch. Do not pull too tight. The knot should resemble a pretzel. Using your thumb to hold everything in place, insert the needle to the right and below the second loop to finish the knot. Do not pull too tight.

**4** Your knot should now look like an X with a double knot in the center.

# No Boundaries

This stitch looks great in a bunch, close together and overlapped.

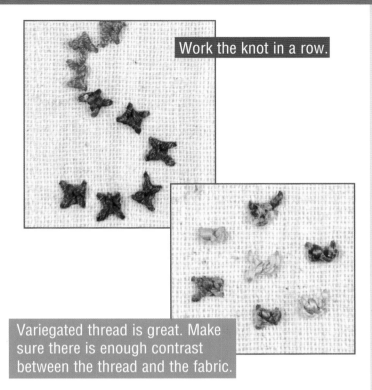

Work the knot in a row.

Variegated thread is great. Make sure there is enough contrast between the thread and the fabric.

Overlap the X part of the stitch.

Work the X part of the stitches in a square to form a box of stitches.

## Tips

- Try to keep the X part of the stitches as close to the same lengths as possible.

- Do not pull the knot too tight; it will distort and won't lay flat.

- Remember to loop the first loop to the left and the second loop to the right.

# Chain Stitches

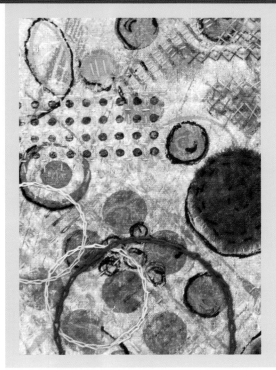

The chain stitch has many variations. It can be curved, detached, layered, opened, twisted, and wrapped. It can be stitched with one or two thin strands of thread or with a heavier fiber that can be pulled through the fabric. If the fiber is too heavy, use a small chain stitch to couch it to the fabric.

*My years of living in Japan are the clear inspiration in the piece on page 68. Small rock and pine tree gardens are prevalent in Japan, but they are almost always hidden behind a fence. As a child it was such a treat to get a glimpse of these gardens. My Japanese garden was stitched using only Valdani threads. The pine needles are variegated silk floss and the rest is is stitched with pearl cottons.*

# Basic Chain Stitch

The chain stitch is basically a backstitch with the thread looped around the needle. When stitched evenly in the traditional way it has the appearance of a linked chain. It can easily be manipulated by lengthening the backstitch or the loop. Lengthening the stitch will give more line while lengthening the loop will add depth.

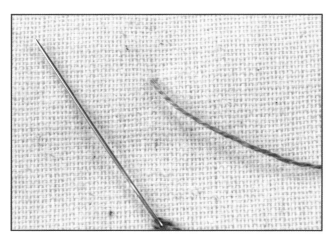

**1** Thread the needle and knot the thread. Bring the needle and thread up from the back of the fabric to the front where you want to begin stitching.

*Note: Remember to keep the needle on top of the fabric while stitching. Working on top of the fabric will limit the number of stitch motions needed, as well as reduce hand fatigue.*

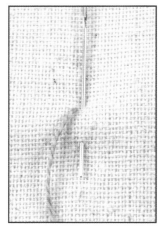

**2** Insert the needle back down into the fabric close to where the thread exited. Bring the needle back up to the top of the fabric 1/4" to 1/2" below the first stitch.

**3** Loop the thread under the needle and pull it through the fabric creating a loop. Take care not to pull the looped thread too tight.

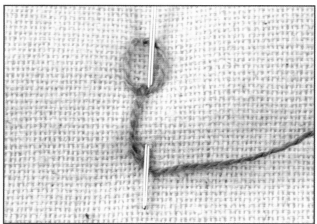

**4** To begin the next stitch, insert the needle inside the loop very close to the thread exit but not in the same hole. Repeat steps 2 – 3 to complete the second chain stitch.

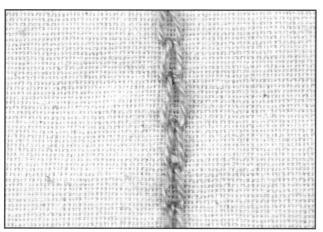

**5** Continue stitching until the row is the length desired. When you are finished stitching, take the needle and thread to the back of the fabric and knot.

# Curved Chain Stitch

The curved chain stitch can be used to create a gentle or sharp curve. Keep in mind that as the curve gets sharper the stitch will become the smaller. The loop may also begin to lose its shape on a sharp curve.

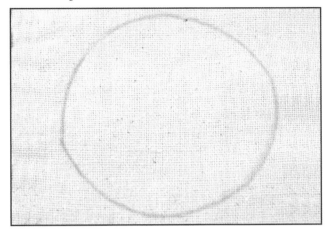

**1** Draw a curved line or circle on the fabric using a fabric marking pencil. Practice with a gentle curve or circle before trying a sharp curve.

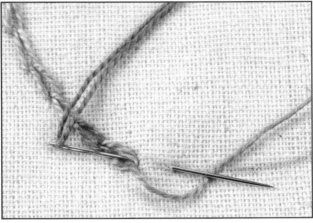

**2** Thread the needle and knot the thread. Bring the needle and thread up from the back of the fabric to the front where you want to begin stitching. Stitch chain stitches along the curved line.

*Note:* Remember to keep the needle on top of the fabric while stitching. Working on top of the fabric will limit the number of stitch motions needed, as well as reduce hand fatigue.

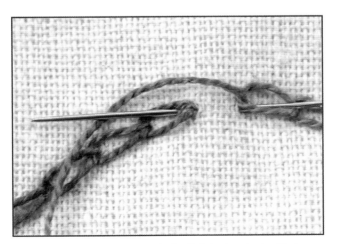

**3** To complete a circle finish the last stitch inside the chain loop of the first stitch. When you are finished stitching, take the needle and thread to the back of the fabric and knot.

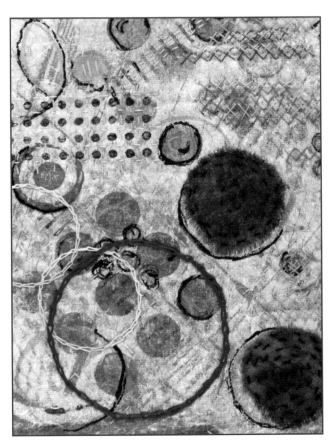

# Detached Chain Stitch

Detached chain stitches are not sewn in a row. Since the stitches aren't attached to one another they can be stitched in any direction.

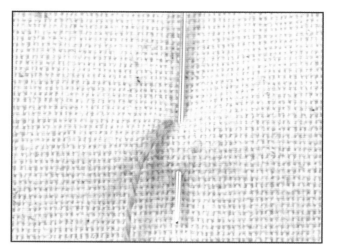

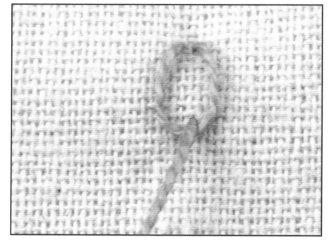

**1** Thread the needle and knot the thread. Bring the needle and thread up from the back of the fabric to the front where you want to begin stitching. Insert the needle back down into the fabric close to where the thread exited, bringing the needle back up to the top of the fabric 1/4" to 1/2" below the thread exit.

**2** Loop the thread under the needle and pull it through the fabric creating a loop. Take care not to pull the looped thread too tight.

*Note:* *Remember to keep the needle on top of the fabric while stitching. Working on top of the fabric will limit the number of stitch motions needed, as well as reduce hand fatigue.*

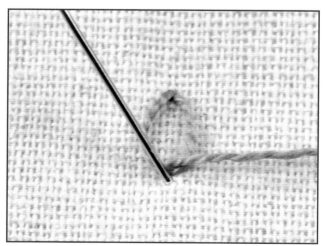

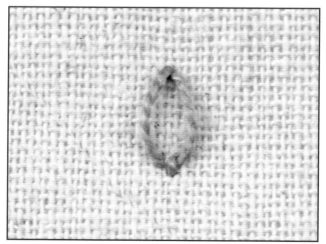

**3** Secure the stitch by inserting the needle down into the fabric just outside the loop.

**4** If you are making a series of detached chain stitches, it is not necessary to knot each time if the individual stitches are close together.

# No Boundaries

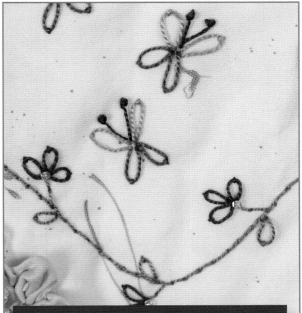

Create leaves, flowers, and butterflies using the detached chain stitch. The flowers and butterflies can also be made using the daisy chain stitch on page 94.

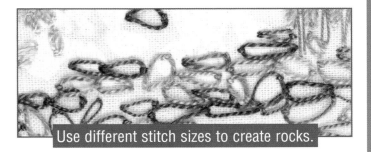

Use different stitch sizes to create rocks.

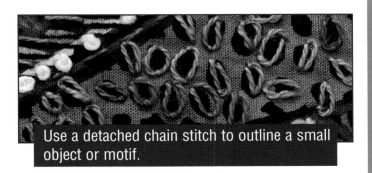

Use a detached chain stitch to outline a small object or motif.

Use a variety of thread weights and colors when grouping the detached chain stitches.

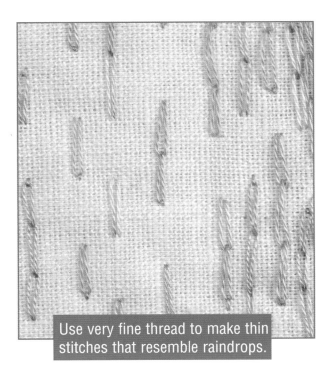

Use very fine thread to make thin stitches that resemble raindrops.

## Tips

- Do not make the loop too long or you will have trouble keeping it round.

- Keep the securing stitch as close to the exit stitch as possible to avoid a tail.

- These stitches can be any size desired.

- Use your thumb to control the loop.

# Layered Chain Stitch

A layered chain stitch is used to give extra depth and added texture by layering different weights and types of fiber. When stitched on top of a grid it becomes a fence, screen or even a grate. Try stitching with a small chain and making each subsequent chain larger to create leaves or wings. It is especially effective with variegated thread or floss.

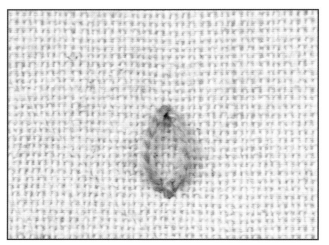

**1** Thread the needle and knot the thread. Bring the needle and thread up from the back of the fabric to the front where you want to begin stitching. Make a small detached chain stitch (page 72).

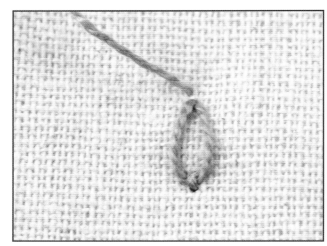

**2** Bring the needle and thread back up to the front of the fabric behind the first stitch.

*Note: Remember to keep the needle on top of the fabric while stitching. Working on top of the fabric will limit the number of stitch motions needed, as well as reduce hand fatigue.*

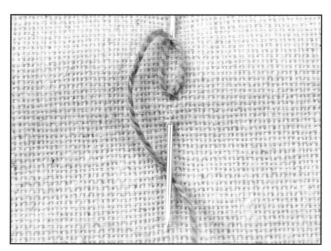

**3** Insert the needle down into the fabric close to where the thread exited. Bring it back up a small space beyond the end of the small detached chain stitch.

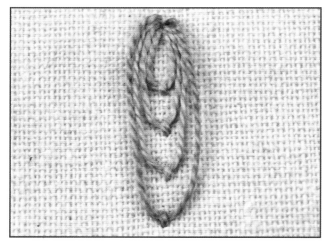

**4** Continue to make each stitch a little larger to surround the previous stitch. Repeat until desired layers are complete.

# No Boundaries

Create fun butterfly wings using bright colored or variegated thread.

Green thread makes great leaves.

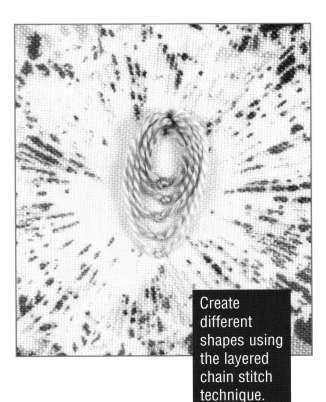

Create different shapes using the layered chain stitch technique.

## Tips

- Remember to allow space around the beginning of the stitch since you will be progressively making the stitch larger.

- Do not pull the thread too tight; it needs to lay flat.

- Use thinner thread if you wish to add several layers.

# Open Chain Stitch

The open chain stitch resembles a ladder stitch. It is used when a curved look is desired. Instead of bringing the needle directly up in front of the stitch it is brought up to the side. It helps to hold the loop with your thumb as the needle is pulled through. In order for the stitch steps to show clearly, we did not use hands in the photos.

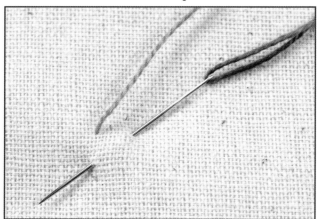

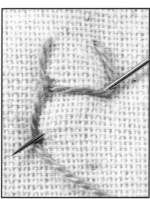

**1** Thread the needle and knot the thread. Bring the needle and thread up from the back of the fabric to the front where you want to begin stitching. Insert the needle back down into the fabric approximately 1/4" to the right of where the thread exited, bringing needle out approximately 1/4" below the thread exit.

**2** Loop the thread under the needle and pull until the loop is the desired size. Keep your thumb on the thread loop and do not pull too tight.

**3** Insert the needle on the right inside of the loop and bring it back up 1/4" below the left side of the loop.

*Note: Remember to keep the needle on top of the fabric while stitching. Working on top of the fabric will limit the number of stitch motions needed, as well as reduce hand fatigue.*

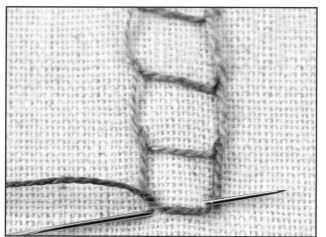

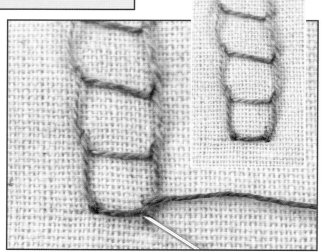

**4** Continue stitching until the row is the length desired. Insert the needle on the left outside of the loop. Bring the needle back up on the right inside of the loop.

**5** Secure the last stitch with a small stitch just outside the right side of the loop.

# No Boundaries

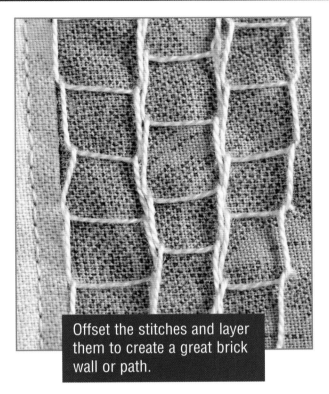

Offset the stitches and layer them to create a great brick wall or path.

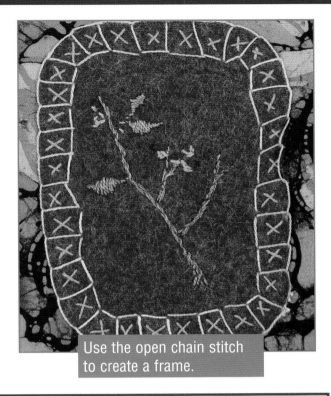

Use the open chain stitch to create a frame.

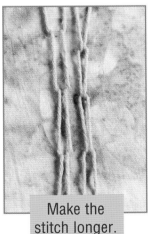

Make the stitch longer.

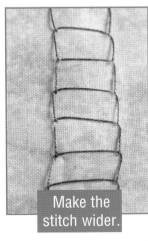

Make the stitch wider.

## Tips

- Take your time and be sure to keep your thumb on the thread.

- There is no set length or width for the stitch.

- Keep the loop loose until the stitch is complete, then adjust it.

*Ruth says*

*Shorten stitches*

# Seed Stitch

The seed stitch, often referred to as ricing, is traditionally stitched with a straight stitch. However, if a chain stitch is used the seeding stitch will cover a little more area. If a thin thread or single strand of floss is used it will resemble the ricing stitch. If a thicker thread or floss is used the seed stitch will stand out more. Each stitch is detached from the others and stitched in a random style. The seed stitch adds texture and interest to a project and can be used to cover large empty spaces.

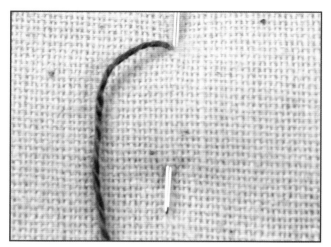

**1** Thread the needle and knot the thread. Bring the needle and thread up from the back of the fabric to the front where you want to begin stitching. Insert the needle back down into the fabric close to the thread exit. Bring the needle back up to the top of the fabric below the first stitch. The seed stitch can be any length you choose.

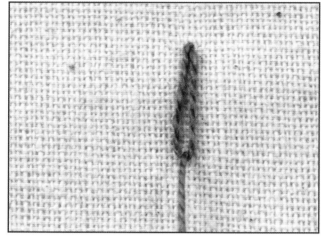

**2** Loop the thread under the needle and pull it through the fabric.

*Note:* *Remember to keep the needle on top of the fabric while stitching. Working on top of the fabric will limit the number of stitch motions needed, as well as reduce hand fatigue.*

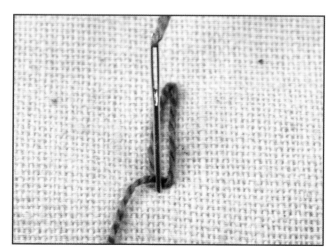

**3** Secure the stitch by inserting the needle down into the fabric just outside the loop.

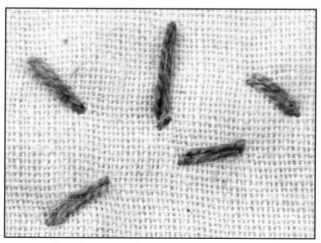

**4** Continue to make a series of seed stitches. When you are finished stitching, take the needle and thread to the back of the fabric and knot.

# No Boundaries

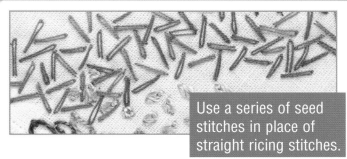

Use a series of seed stitches in place of straight ricing stitches.

Create the seed stitches with heavier thread weights for a more textured look.

## Tips

- Use a very fine thread to create a ricing look with a chain stitch.

- Keep the exit and entrance of the thread as close together as possible.

- Use the seed stitch to cover large areas.

- Mix the thread weights and colors to add interest.

*Designer Gallery*

**Interpreting the Tree of Life by Venisa Gallegos**

Stitch used was a split backstitch.

# Twisted Chain Stitch

The twisted chain stitch requires an extra twisting of the thread on the needle. The loop is twisted before the needle goes back down into the fabric. Hold the loop loosely with the thumb while making each stitch.

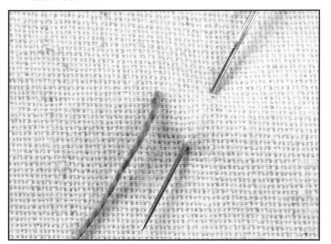

**1** Thread the needle and knot the thread. Bring the needle and thread up from the back of the fabric to the front where you want to begin stitching. Insert the needle back down into the fabric approximately 1/4" to the side of the thread exit. Bring the needle back up to the front of the fabric in the center and approximately 1/4" below the first two stitches.

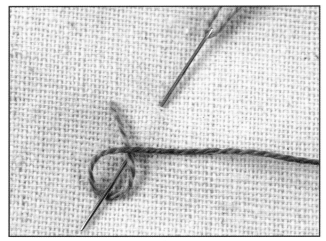

**2** Loop the thread over and then under the needle creating a 'twist'.

> *Note:* *Remember to keep the needle on top of the fabric while stitching. Working on top of the fabric will limit the number of stitch motions needed, as well as reduce hand fatigue.*

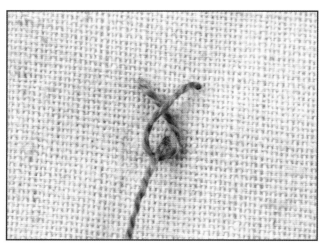

**3** Holding the loop loosely with your thumb, pull the needle and thread through the fabric to create the twisted chain stitch. In order for the stitch steps to show clearly, we did not use hands in the photos.

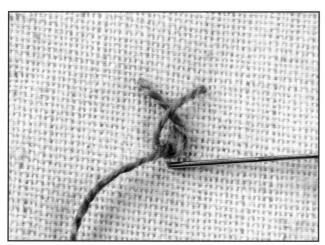

**4** Secure the stitch by inserting the needle down into the fabric just outside the loop. If you are making a series of twisted chain stitches that are close together, it is not necessary to knot each individual.

# No Boundaries

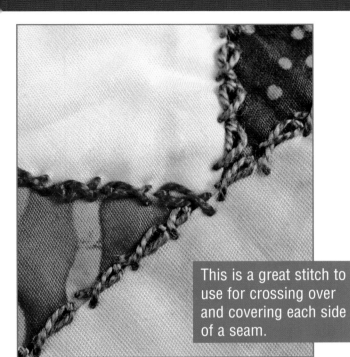

This is a great stitch to use for crossing over and covering each side of a seam.

Change the weight of the threads as you work each row.

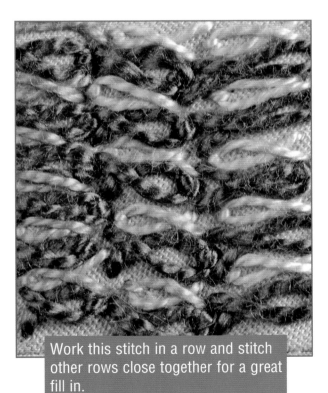

Separate the stitches to create fish.

Work this stitch in a row and stitch other rows close together for a great fill in.

## Tips

- Work on a flat surface. This will help keep the loops twisted.

- Do not pull too tight or the stitch will pucker.

- The twist can be worked either to the left or right.

# Wrapped Chain Stitch

The wrapped chain stitch begins with a row of basic chain stitches. Another thread or fiber is then woven through the row to create the wrapped chain stitch.

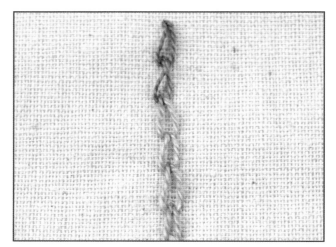

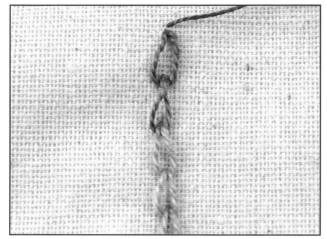

**1** Thread the needle and knot the thread. Bring the needle and thread up from the back of the fabric to the front where you want to begin stitching. Stitch a row of basic chain stitches. Take the needle and thread to the back when you are finished stitching and knot.

**2** Using a second thread or fiber, thread the needle and knot the thread. Bring the needle and thread up from the back of the fabric to the front at the beginning of the chain.

*Note: Remember to keep the needle on top of the fabric while stitching. Working on top of the fabric will limit the number of stitch motions needed, as well as reduce hand fatigue.*

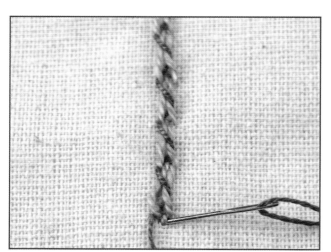

**3** Weave the thread around the chain without stitching through the fabric. Refer to No Boundaries for other ways to wrap the row of chain stitches.

**4** When you reach the end of the chain, take the needle and thread to the back and knot.

# No Boundaries

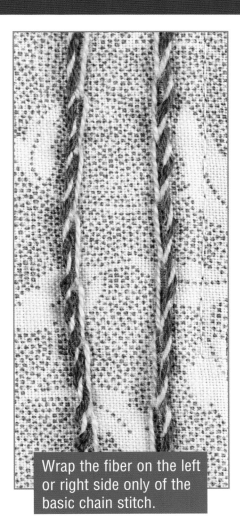

Mix it up and wrap both sides and the entire stitch in the same chain.

Wrap the fiber on the left or right side only of the basic chain stitch.

Wrap the fiber through the entire row of basic chain stitches.

## Tips

- Use a contrasting thread to wrap the row of basic chain stitches.

- Use a metallic thread for wrapping. Metallic threads have a tendency to ravel when pulled through fabric so using it to wrap eliminates that issue.

- Make your row of basic chain stitches even so the wrapping appears even.

# Zigzag Chain Stitch

The zigzag chain stitch is a fun way to stitch movement into your work. Instead of chain stitching in a straight line move each chain stitch back and forth in a zigzag pattern.

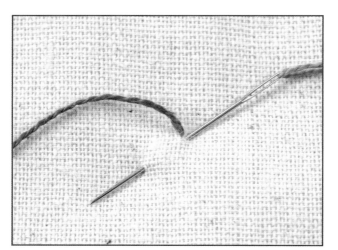

**1** Thread the needle and knot the thread. Bring the needle and thread up from the back of the fabric to the front where you want to begin stitching. Insert the needle back down into the fabric close to where the thread exited. Bring the needle back up to the top of the fabric 1/4" to 1/2" to the left or right of the thread exit.

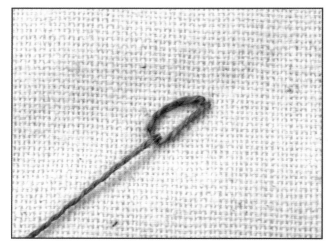

**2** Loop the thread under the needle and pull it through the fabric creating a loop. Take care not to pull the looped thread too tight.

> *Note:* *Remember to keep the needle on top of the fabric while stitching. Working on top of the fabric will limit the number of stitch motions needed, as well as reduce hand fatigue.*

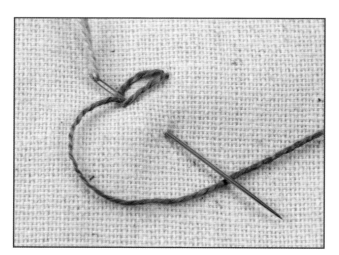

**3** To begin the next stitch, insert the needle inside the loop very close to the thread exit but not in the same hole. Bring the needle back up to the top of the fabric 1/4" to 1/2" to the opposite side of the first stitch.

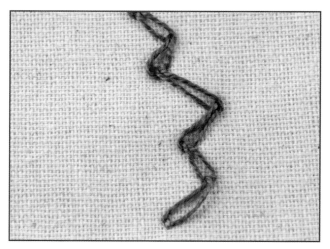

**4** Continue stitching until the row of chain zigzag stitches is the length desired. When you are finished stitching, secure the stitch by inserting the needle down into the fabric just outside the loop.

# No Boundaries

Try stitching in rows butted up to one another.

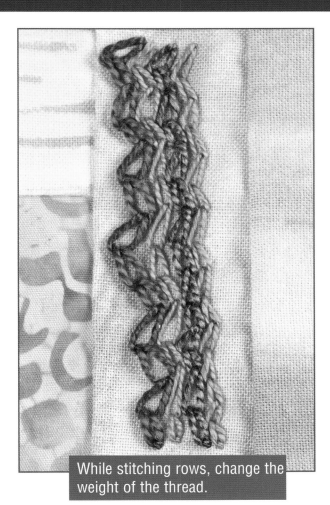

While stitching rows, change the weight of the thread.

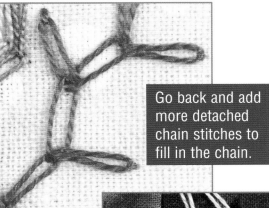

Go back and add more detached chain stitches to fill in the chain.

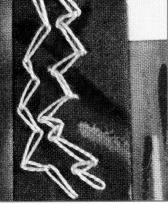

Change the length of the stitch.

## Tips

- When zigzagging, be careful not to lay the stitch down at too shallow of an angle or it will begin to get loose.

- Do not pull the threads too tight. This is an easy mistake to make when working at an angle.

# Double Chain Stitch

The double chain stitch is a half open chain worked with two chains together. It is important to keep your thumb on the thread as you work.

*Note: In order for the stitch steps to show clearly, we did not use hands in the photos.*

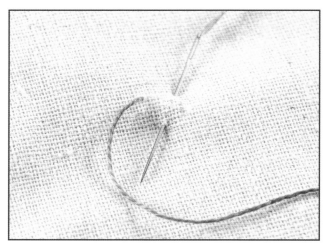

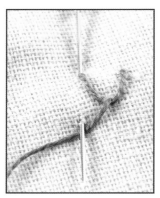

**1** Thread the needle and knot the thread. Bring the needle and thread up from the back of the fabric to the front where you want to begin stitching. Insert the needle back down into the fabric approximately 1/4" to the right of the thread exit, bringing the needle back up in the center and approximately 1/4" below the stitch to form a V.

**2** Loop the thread under the needle and pull through. You now have a stitch that looks like a fly stitch.

**3** Insert the needle back down into the fabric at the thread exit of the first stitch. Bring the needle back up approximately 1/4" below the stitch.

*Note: Remember to keep the needle on top of the fabric while stitching. Working on top of the fabric will limit the number of stitch motions needed, as well as reduce hand fatigue.*

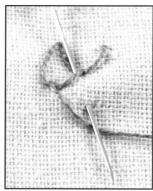

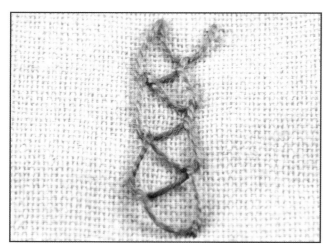

**4** Loop thread under the needle and pull through.

**5** Continue working back and forth to create a side-by-side partially open chain.

**6** When you are finished stitching, secure the stitch by inserting the needle down into the fabric just outside the loop.

# No Boundaries

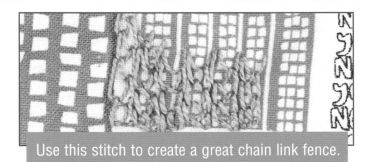

Use this stitch to create a great chain link fence.

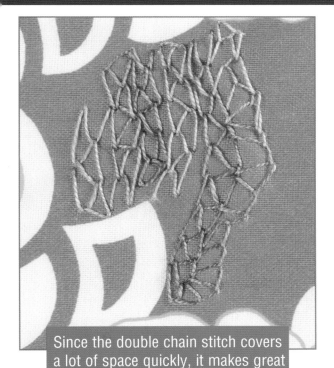

Since the double chain stitch covers a lot of space quickly, it makes great background texture.

Variegated threads look wonderful with the double chain stitch.

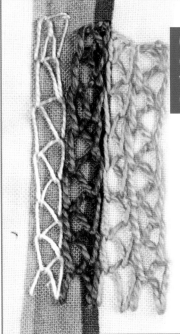

Create rows next to each other using different weights of thread for great texture.

## Tips

- Be careful not to pull the stitch too tight or the thread will bunch up.

- Use your thumb to control the looping of the thread.

- Try to enter and exit the fabric as close to the previous stitch as possible.

# Cable Chain Stitch

The cable chain stitch is a simple stitch that gives the appearance of a linked chain.

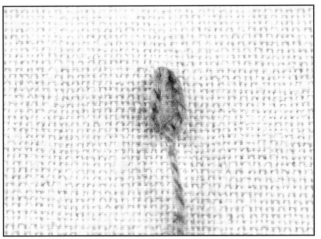

**1** Thread the needle and knot the thread. Bring the needle and thread up from the back of the fabric to the front where you want to begin stitching. Stitch one chain stitch (page 70).

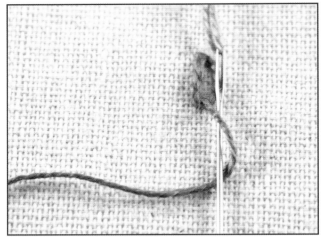

**2** Referring to the photo, wrap the thread around the needle once.

*Note: Remember to keep the needle on top of the fabric while stitching. Working on top of the fabric will limit the number of stitch motions needed, as well as reduce hand fatigue.*

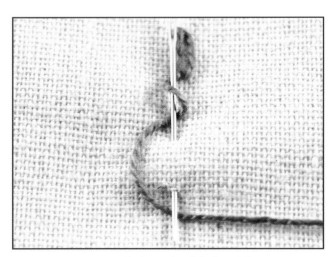

**3** Insert needle into the fabric 1/4" to 1" in front of the first chain stitch and make another.

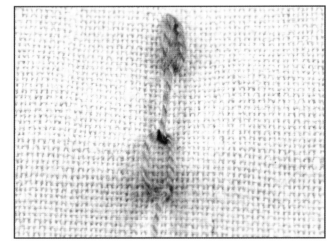

**4** Pull the needle and thread through the fabric. You will have a chain stitch with a straight stitch in between. Continue stitching until the row is the length desired. This will give a linked chain appearance.

# No Boundaries

Vary the lengths of both chain and link in the same row of stitches.

Vary the chain length.

Vary the link length.

## Tips

- Loop the thread the same direction for each stitch if you want it to look consistent. If this is not important to you, don't worry about it.

- Do not pull the thread too tight on the chain or the link as this will distort and pucker the fabric.

- Be sure to let the chain section look fuller than the link section or it will not look like a chain and link.

- The cable chain stitch can be made or large depending on its use—large for a ship's anchor chain or small for a necklace.

# Detached Loop Chain Stitch

The detached loop chain stitch allows the loop section of the stitch to hang free on one side to create a 3-D effect.

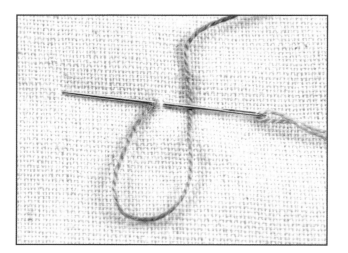

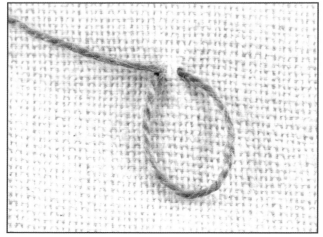

**1** Thread the needle and knot the thread. Bring the needle and thread up from the back of the fabric to the front where you want to begin stitching. Make a loop with the thread. Take a very small stitch at the top of the loop and close to the thread exit.

**2** Pull the thread through until the loop is the desired size. Hold the loop loosely with your thumb as you pull.

*Note: Remember to keep the needle on top of the fabric while stitching. Working on top of the fabric will limit the number of stitch motions needed, as well as reduce hand fatigue.*

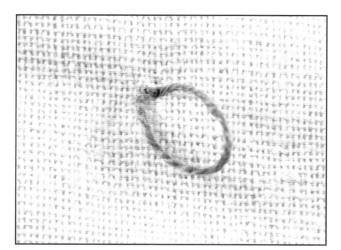

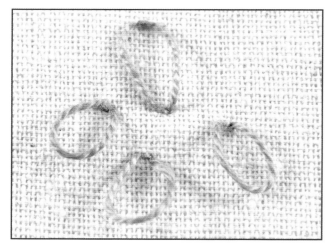

**3** Insert the needle back down into the fabric as close to the top of the loop as possible. Secure the stitch by knotting the thread.

**4** If you are making a series of detached loop chain stitches, it is not necessary to knot each time if the individual stitches are close together.

# No Boundaries

Use the loops for attaching found objects.

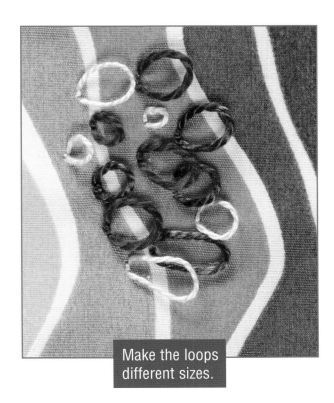

Make the loops different sizes.

Stitch the loops in rows.

## Tips

- Take the smallest stitch possible at the top of the loop.

- Control the loop thread with your thumb whenever possible.

- Do not pull the small stitches too tight. They are so close together they may pop through to the back.

- Detached loop chain stitches make great fur or hair.

# Coral Chain Stitch

The coral chain stitch resembles a zigzag with a knot at each "joint". The size of the knot will depend on the weight of the thread or fiber used.

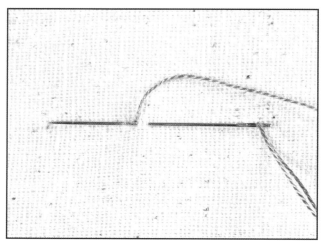

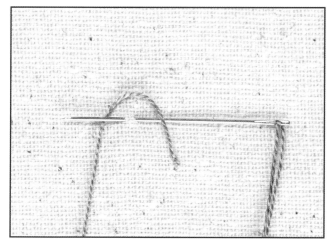

**1** Thread the needle and knot the thread. Bring the needle and thread up from the back of the fabric to the front where you want to begin stitching. Take a small stitch close to where the thread exited.

**2** Take another small stitch 1/4" – 1/2" above and to the left of the first stitch. Loop the thread over and under the needle as shown. Pull the needle and thread through to form a knot.

*Note:* *Remember to keep the needle on top of the fabric while stitching. Working on top of the fabric will limit the number of stitch motions needed, as well as reduce hand fatigue.*

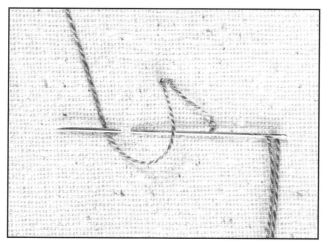

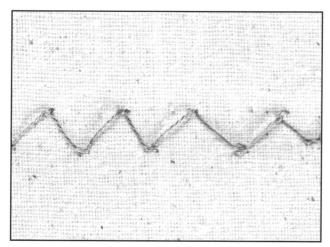

**3** Continue making stitches in a zigzag (left to right to left) manner.

**4** When the row is the length desired, take the needle and thread to the back of the fabric and knot.

# No Boundaries

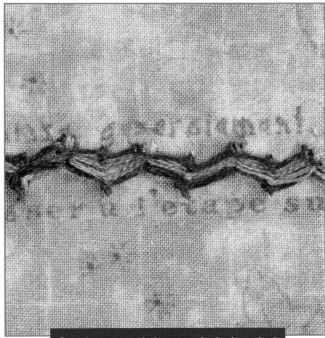

Stack rows of the coral chain stitch.

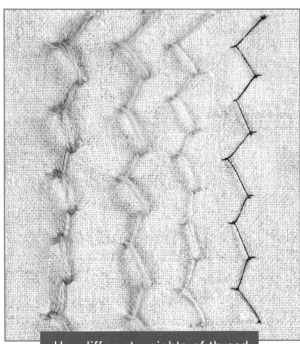

Use different weights of thread.

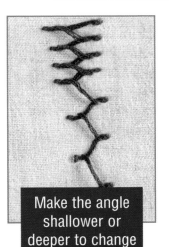

Make the angle shallower or deeper to change the zigzag.

Loop the thread around the needle more than once for a bigger knot.

## Tips

- Keep the small stitches as small as possible so the knot shows better.

- Do not pull the knot too tight or it will look like a messy stitch.

*Ruth says*

*Change weights*

# Daisy Chain Stitch

The daisy chain stitch, also known as the lazy daisy stitch, is a detached chain stitch worked in a circle. It is one of the easiest stitches to learn.

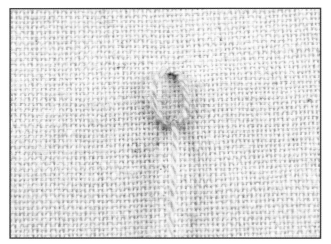

**1** Thread the needle and knot the thread. Bring the needle and thread up from the back of the fabric to the front where you want the center of the 'daisy'. Make a detached chain stitch.

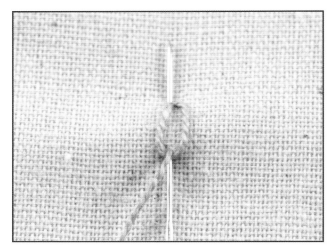

**2** Secure the stitch on the outside of the loop. Bring the needle back up to the top of the fabric next to the beginning of the first stitch.

*Note: Remember to keep the needle on top of the fabric while stitching. Working on top of the fabric will limit the number of stitch motions needed, as well as reduce hand fatigue.*

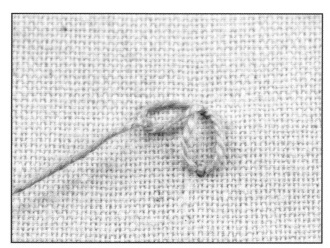

**3** Make another detached chain stitch slightly to the side of the first so the beginning stitches are close together but the ends of the stitches are farther apart.

**4** Continue working in a circle until the "daisy" is complete. When you are finished stitching, take the needle and thread to the back of the fabric and knot.

# No Boundaries

The flower doesn't have to be a daisy, try using fine thread and many petals and it will make a chrysanthemum.

Long thin stitches in one direction instead of a circle will make a bud.

Vary the length and width of the stitches for a more organic look to the flower. Nature is not always symmetrical.

Go back over the stitches and fill in to create fuller bushes, leaves, or flowers.

Make a small daisy and then go back and make a larger one around it.

Use a French knot for the centers.

## Tips

- To begin, make all the stitches the same size.

- It is easier to space the daisy petals evenly by stitching 3 petals with space between them and then going back and filling in with more petals.

- Keep the middle beginning stitches as close to the center as possible.

# Stacked Chain Stitch

The stacked chain stitch is a group of horizontal detached chain stitches. It is stitched in one direction and then the other.

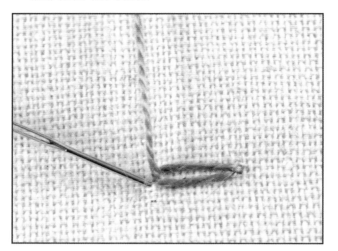

**1** Thread the needle and knot the thread. Bring the needle and thread up from the back of the fabric to the front where you want to begin stitching. Make a horizontal detached chain stitch, securing it with a small stitch on the outside of the loop.

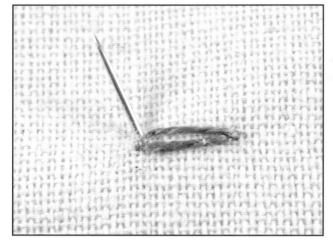

**2** Bring the needle back up to the top of the fabric above the securing stitch of the first stitch.

*Note: Remember to keep the needle on top of the fabric while stitching. Working on top of the fabric will limit the number of stitch motions needed, as well as reduce hand fatigue.*

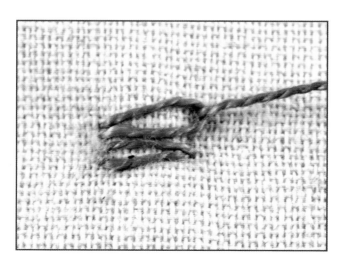

**3** Make another horizontal detached chain stitch, stitching in the opposite direction.

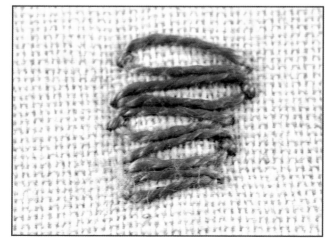

**4** Continue stitching until the row is the length desired. When you are finished stitching, take the needle and thread to the back of the fabric and knot.

# No Boundaries

Vary the length of the horizontal detached chain stitch.

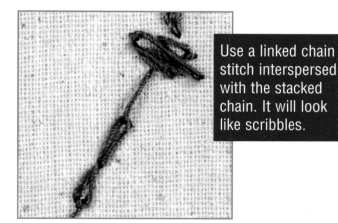

Use a linked chain stitch interspersed with the stacked chain. It will look like scribbles.

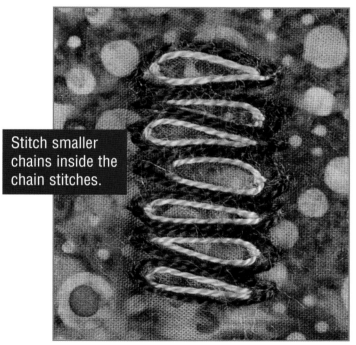

Stitch smaller chains inside the chain stitches.

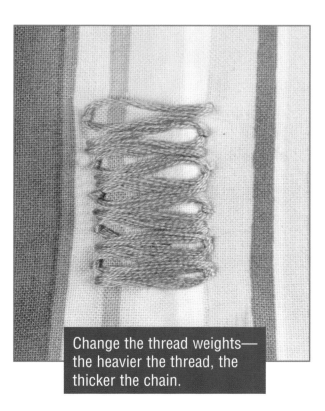

Change the thread weights—the heavier the thread, the thicker the chain.

## Tips

- Switch the directions of the stitches for a smoother finish.

- Do not pull the thread too tight or the loop will become more of a line.

- Use your thumb to control the thread tightness.

### The Lady with the Birds by Judy Gula

Stitches used include stem stitch, backstitch, chain stitch, French knot and daisy chain stitch.

### Man Goes to Catch Fish by Liz Kettle

Stitches used include straight stitch, running stitch and ricing.

**Summer Surprise by Deb Prewitt**
Stitches used include ricing, French knots and couching

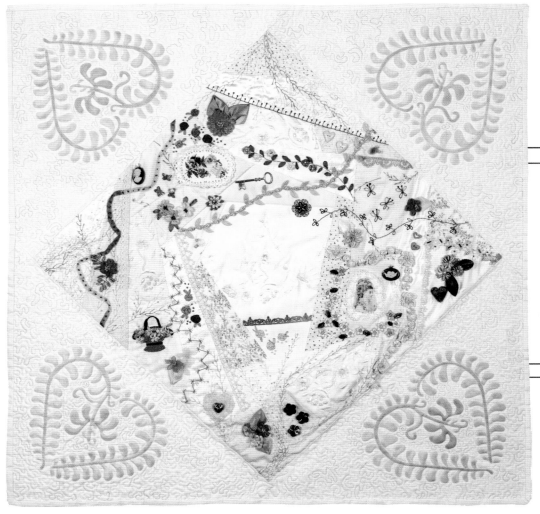

## Crazy Wedding Challenge
by Kerry Cain

Stitches used include straight stitch, backstitch, buttonhole stitch, herringbone stitch, feather stitch, French knot, daisy chain stitch and couching.

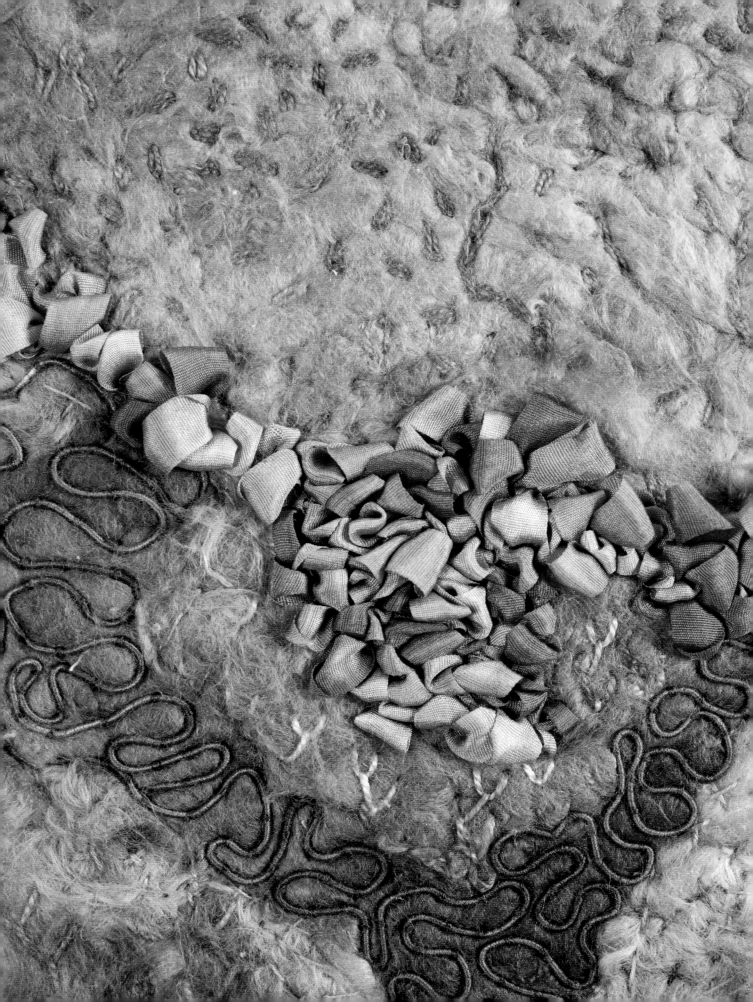

# Couching & Wrapping

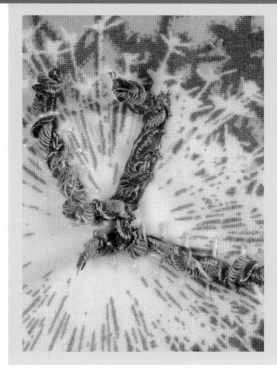

Couching and wrapping are techniques that allow you to attach heavy threads and fibers to your projects without repeatedly pulling the fibers through the fabric. In this section, you will use many of the stitches you have already learned to couch and wrap the fibers.

*In the piece on page 100, I wanted to demonstrate how couching can cover large areas of fiber. The silk ribbon is couched by leaving it looped up and loose instead of flat, creating a 3-D or textured look. There is more than four yards of ribbon on this piece. The ribbon, silk hankies, and roving are from Treenway Silks. The blue gimp and other threads are from Tentakulum with a bit of Valdani pearl cotton stitched at the top.*

# Couching

Couching is a technique used to attach heavy threads and thicker fibers to fabric. Rather than stitching with them, another thread is used to secure them to the fabric. Traditionally a small stitch is used to couch the fiber, with great care being taken to hide the stitch.

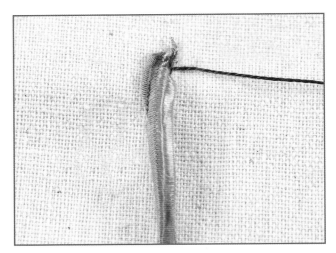

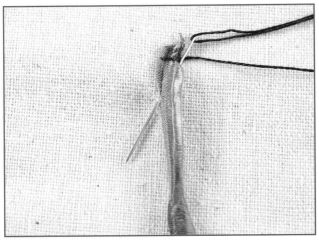

**1** Place the fiber to be couched on the fabric in the position desired. Thread the needle and knot the thread. Bring the needle and thread up from the back of the fabric at one end and as close to the fiber as possible.

**2** Loop the thread over the fiber and enter the fabric as close to the exit stitch as possible, bringing the needle up approximately 1/2" below the first stitch. Pull through.

*Note:* Remember to keep the needle on top of the fabric while stitching. Working on top of the fabric will limit the number of stitch motions needed, as well as reduce hand fatigue.

*Keep the fiber in place as you are stitching. This photo illustrates needle position only.*

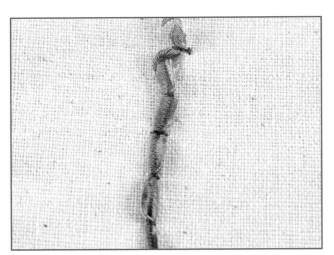

**3** Loop the thread over the fiber and insert the needle into the fabric as close to the exit stitch as possible. Bring the needle and thread back up approximately 1/2" below the first stitch. Pull through.

**4** Continue couching in this manner until the fiber is completely attached.

# No Boundaries

The couched fiber does not always have to lay flat. Try pulling it up to achieve a 3-D effect.

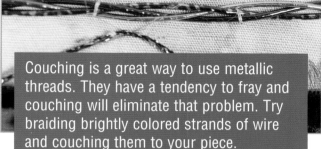

Couching is a great way to use metallic threads. They have a tendency to fray and couching will eliminate that problem. Try braiding brightly colored strands of wire and couching them to your piece.

Couching can be used to attach found items, such as a washer or twig.

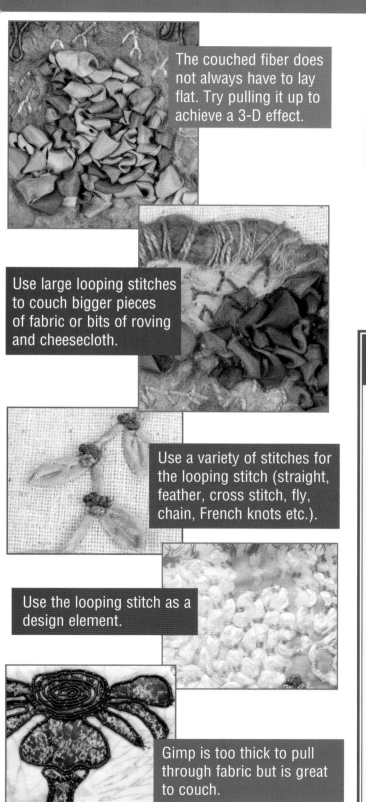

Use large looping stitches to couch bigger pieces of fabric or bits of roving and cheesecloth.

Use a variety of stitches for the looping stitch (straight, feather, cross stitch, fly, chain, French knots etc.).

Use the looping stitch as a design element.

Gimp is too thick to pull through fabric but is great to couch.

## Tips

- To make the securing stitch invisible use 100-weight silk thread in a neutral color.

- Do not pull the looping thread so tight that it bunches the fiber being couched.

- Keep the looping stitches evenly spaced. You can also make them uneven for an added design element.

- If the couching fiber is being curved, space the looping stitches closer together.

- When a thread or fiber is too heavy to pull through the fabric, couching it is a good solution.

- It is easier to thread ribbon through the eye of a needle if it is cut at an angle.

- After some practice, you will be able to exit and enter the fabric in one motion.

# Wrapping

Wrapping is a technique used when the fiber is too heavy to be pulled repeatedly through the fabric. Instead of using a looping thread to secure the fiber, the heavier fiber is wrapped around a row or group of stitches. The heavier fiber will need to be pulled through the fabric at the beginning and end of the wrap, so choose a fiber with that in mind. If the fiber is too heavy to pull through the fabric, the knot will need to lie on top of the fabric. The knot will be visible, but can be incorporated into the overall design.

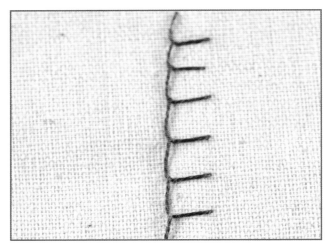

**1** Stitch a row of blanket, chain, straight, or backstitches.

*Note: After wrapping a row of stitches, experiment with wrapping a group of stitches (fly, cross stitches, etc.)*

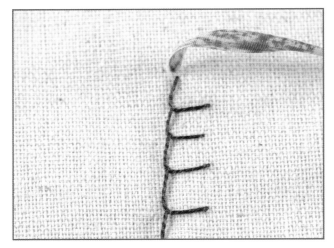

**2** Thread the needle with the wrapping thread or fiber and knot it. Bring the needle and wrapping fiber up from the back of the fabric at the beginning of the stitch row.

*Note: Remember to keep the needle on top of the fabric while stitching. Working on top of the fabric will limit the number of stitch motions needed, as well as reduce hand fatigue.*

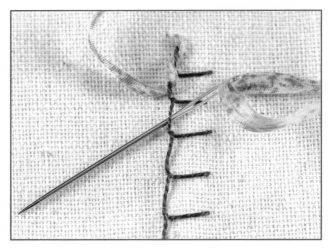

**3** Without piercing the fabric wrap the fiber in and out of the stitched row.

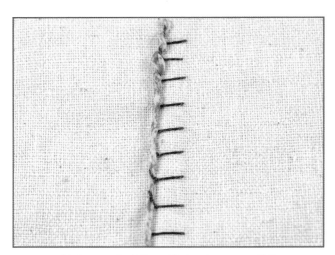

**4** At the end of the stitched row, pull the wrapping fiber to the back of fabric and knot.

# No Boundaries

Use as an outline to make a design stand out.

Create several stitch rows close together and wrap them together.

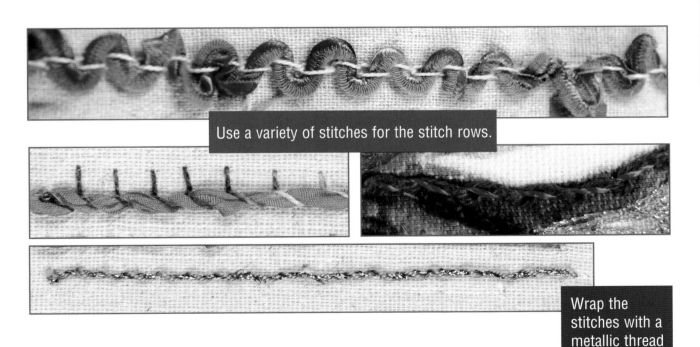

Use a variety of stitches for the stitch rows.

Wrap the stitches with a metallic thread to add sparkle to a design.

# Finishing the Stitch Sampler Book

## Supplies

7 yards assorted fibers for trim

1 yard of ribbon for closure

Button for front closure

5" piece of ribbon to attach button

Fabric marking pencil

Sewing machine

Couching feet (optional)

Thread to blend with trim

Needles of varying sizes to correspond with the fibers

Thimble

Scissors

## Stitching the Cover

Before putting the stitch sampler book together, you will need to hand stitch the front cover. I used a variety of stitches for my sampler cover and labeled it Stitch Play. Embellish your sampler cover with your favorite stitches or a random design—it's your book, do whatever you like. The button closure will be centered approximately 1" from the edge, so you may want to avoid stitching this small area.

## Cutting and Assembly

From assorted fibers, cut:
>    10—14" lengths and 2—45" lengths for trim.

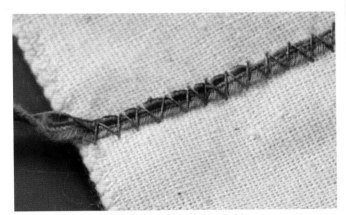

**1** Lay 14" fibers over the 8 vertical section divisions marked on the stitch sampler. The two ends will remain open.

**2** Using a zigzag, straight, or decorative programmed stitch, machine couch the fibers in place. You may also choose to hand couch the fibers on the sampler. Do not trim the fibers.

**3** Lay a 45" fiber over the marked horizontal section division in the center of the sampler. Machine or hand-couch the fiber. Do not trim the fiber.

**4** Fold the sampler lengthwise, right sides together. The piece should measure approximately 44" x 6-1/2". Take the time to line up the couched fibers. Make sure they are all straight before you begin stitching the piece together.

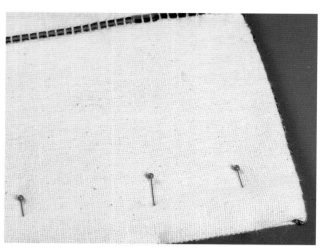

**5** Pin each section along one short end of the sampler where the fibers meet.

**6** Using a straight stitch, stitch along the length of the sampler edges and one short end. Leave one short end open.

**7** Trim, allowing a 1/4" seam allowance. Do not trim the open end yet.

**8** Turn the sampler right side out. Press flat taking care to make the folds straight. Trim the open end 1/4" past the stitch line.

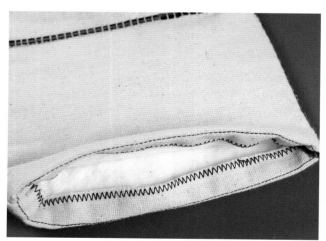

**9** Press the stitched line under. Pin the open end and stitch closed. The sampler should no longer have any raw edges.

**10** Hand-couch the short ends of the sampler with the remaining 14" fibers. I double my fibers on the short ends to make sure I cover the seam.

**11** Hand-couch the bottom edge of the sampler with the remaining 45" fiber. I like to make knots on the ends but you can hide the ends under the couching if you prefer.

**12** Center the button on the cover and approximately 1" in from the edge. Thread a large needle with the 5" piece of ribbon. Take the needle and thread down into one of the button's holes and bring it back up to the top through another hole and tie it off. Trim the ribbon.

**13** Tie the remaining length of ribbon around the button between it and the fabric. Fold your stitch sampler and wrap the ribbon around it to hold it closed.

# Printing Stitch Names on Ribbon

Ribbon printed with the name of each stitch is a creative way to label the pages of your stitch sampler book. To provide a handy reference, print the basic name of the stitch on the ribbon and attach it to the page that shows the basic stitch, as well as several of its variations.

## Supplies

Computer and inkjet printer

Rayon, silk or cotton ribbon; polyester and nylon ribbon can be used but the ink may bleed slightly.

Copy paper

Double-sided tape

*Note: To prevent fraying, paint the cut ribbon ends with clear nail polish.*

**1** In the word processing program on your computer type each stitch name on a separate line. Space the lines to allow for the ribbon width. Print the text on a sheet of copy paper. Do not close the program.

**2** Apply double-sided tape directly on top of the printed words. The tape can be slightly narrower than the ribbon. If the ribbon is very wide use two strips of tape.

**3** Smooth the ribbon onto the tape, taking care not to stretch the ribbon. The double-sided tape should be completely covered by the ribbon so it will not stick to the printer rollers.

**4** Place the paper with the ribbon attached into the printer and print the text again. Allow time for the ink to dry before carefully peeling the ribbon off the tape.

**5** Use the stitch that corresponds to each page to attach the printed ribbon to the sampler book stitch pages.

*Ruth says* → *Use unconventional fibers*

Stitches used include straight stitch, ricing stitch, blanket stitch, cross stitch, feather stitch, fly stitch, chain stitch, French knot, bullion knot and couching.

# About the Author

Ruth Chandler grew up in Japan where the vibrant color and texture of Japanese fabric, combined with the simplicity of Japanese design, caught her attention. Ruth learned basic Sashiko from an elderly neighbor at the age of four, and began to create and sew her own clothes, which became an outlet for her imagination and creativity. She made her first quilt in 1990, a queen size, hand-appliquéd and hand-quilted Hawaiian pineapple quilt; she has never looked back. In her own unique style she loves to use new techniques mingled with the old and her work usually shows the influence of her years spent in Japan.

Ruth teaches locally from her home studio and Blue Twig Studio, and nationally at Art and Soul Retreats. She can also be seen in Open Studios at International Quilt Market and teaches for Make it University. Ruth has written several articles for Quilting Arts magazine and blog posts for Havel's Sewing. Her work has been published in several books including A Fiber Artist's Guide to Color & Design, First-time Beading on Fabric, and Fabric Color Magic. She can also be found at www.textileevolution.com, an online stitch community with free book studies. Ruth is one of the co-authors of the best-selling book, Fabric Embellishing The basics & beyond. She may be contacted for nationwide classes at ruthachandler@comcast.net.

Ruth lives in Colorado Springs, Colorado at the foot of Pikes Peak with her husband of 35 years. She has a daughter and son, both married and 5 beautiful grandchildren who are being introduced to all art forms at a very early age.

# Thank You

I would like to thank my support group, The Full Circle, for keeping me on track, encouraging me and being a great sounding board. Liz, Cass, Deb and Terza, I appreciate all the support you give me on a daily basis.

Thank you to Kreinik Threads, Treenway Silks, Valdani threads, and Tentakulum painter's threads for supplying threads and fibers for this book. You have all been so generous.

Thanks to Havel's® Scissors for supplying terrific, super sharp scissors. I love being able to get such a clean cut; it makes my needle so much easier to thread. My students love the scissors you supply.

Thank you to Roc-Lon® Industries for supplying the Osnaburg fabric for step-by-step photography and the stitch sampler book.

A special thanks to all my amazing friends and students for your incredible support. You are a great bunch of women. An extra special thank you to Liz Kettle, my partner in crime. You can find us both at www.textileevolution.com.

Thanks to the artists who loaned their pieces to be used as inspiration through the book.

Thank you to my husband Greg for your patience. You are my rock!

Finally, I want to thank the crew at Landauer Publishing for their patience and support. I have loved working with all of you over the last five years.

# Resources

Begin at your local quilt and craft stores when purchasing your hand stitching materials. I realize that many of the unique items, such as specialty threads and fibers, are more difficult to find and have listed my favorite on-line stores. All the companies listed have been very supportive and generously supplied the materials needed for this book.

### Artistic Artifacts
Tentakulum threads and fibers
Hand-dyed pieces
Batik panels
Needles and other supplies
www.artisticartifacts.com

### Blue Twig Studio
Valdani threads
Wonderful ribbons
Needles and other supplies
Tentakulum threads and fibers
www.bluetwigstudio.com

### Kreinik Threads
Threads in a range of size and colors,
including fine invisible threads, thick cottons
and wools, silk and metallic.
www.kreinikthreads.com

### Tentakulum
Hand-dyed Painter's threads in cotton, silk and wool
Gimp
Coordinated packs of fibers and fabrics
www.shop.tentakulum.com

### Treenway Silks
Thread, ribbon and yarn collections in silk,
cotton, rayon and wool
Hand-dyed silk roving, cocoons, hankies
and carrier rods
www.treenwaysilks.com

### Valdani Threads
Assortment of hand-dyed pearl cotton, pearl silk, silk
floss, cotton floss, crochet cotton and yarns
www.valdani.com

## *The following artists' work appears as inspiration throughout the book.*

### Barbara Allen
barb.allen.artquilts@gmail.com
Take Two... - page 14 with close-ups on pages 23, 29, 31, 33, 35, 45, 77

### Kerry Cain
kcainco@yahoo.com
Pictographs Interpreted - page 63 with close-ups on pages 29, 61

Crazy Wedding Challenge - page 99 with close-ups on pages 33, 73

### Venisa M. Gallegos
Interpreting the Tree of Life - page 79 with close-up on page 23

### Judy Gula
www.ArtisticArtifacts.com
The Lady with the Birds - page 98 with close-ups on pages 17, 25, 27, 61, 73

Orchid by Wooden Printing Block - page 15 with close-ups on pages 25, 61, 103

### Liz Kettle
www.textileevolution.com
A Man Goes to Catch Fish - page 98 with close-ups on pages 19, 21, 27

Connections - page 49 with close-ups on pages 45, 69, 71

### Cass Mullane
www.CassMullane.com
Textures 3 - page 54 with close-ups on pages 21, 27, 37, 59, 61, 65, 79

### Deb Prewitt
www.bluetwigstudio.com
Summer Surprise - page 99 with close-up on page 103

The stitch section openers on pages 16, 30, 40, 58, 68, and 100 were created by Ruth Chandler, as well as Metamorphosis on page 110 with close-ups on pages 23, 25, 29, 53 and 103. Her work is also shown in several of the No Boundaries photographs throughout the book.